John,

With grateful thanks and
very best wishes

John

# Postal Performance

## The Transformation of a Global Industry

JOHN M. DOWSON,
EDWARD E. HORGAN, JR.
T. WOOD PARKER

Copyright © 1997 by Coopers & Lybrand L.L.P.

Coopers & Lybrand L.L.P., 1530 Wilson Blvd., Arlington, VA 22209

All rights reserved. Printed in the United States of America. Except as permitted under the United States Copyright Act of 1976, no part of this publication may be reproduced or distributed in any form or by any means, or stored in a data base or retrieval system, without the prior written permission of Coopers & Lybrand.

John M. Dowson, Edward E. Horgan, Jr. and T. Wood Parker

Postal Performance: The Transformation of a Global Industry

Library of Congress Catalog No. 96-085783

ISBN 0-944533-23X

Bulk quantities of this book may be obtained from:

Bookmasters, Inc.
Distribution Center
1444 State Rt. 42
RD 11
Mansfield, Ohio 44903
Telephone: 1-800-247-6553
Fax: 419-281-6883

# TABLE OF CONTENTS

*"To Ruth and Duncan, who put up with my long hours and with whom I share great fun."*

— John Dowson

*"To Eileen, my inspiration and partner in life."*

— Ed Horgan

*"To Emmy, my best friend, for her understanding and support."*

— Wood Parker

# ACKNOWLEDGEMENTS

The themes of this book are rooted in the consulting work we have done with dozens of organizations both within and outside the global postal industry. Some of these organizations are at the leading edge of transformation. Others are striving to embrace change for the first time. We are deeply indebted to all of them — and to the many outstanding executives who manage them — for inspiring us to think in new and transformational ways.

Our insights were especially enriched by our dialogue with executives from the world's postal administrations and postal industry leaders during the year we spent researching and writing this book. For their conversations and perspectives, we'd like to particularly thank: Laurel Kamen, Vice-President, American Express; Alan Goddard, Director, An Post; John Hynes, Chief Executive Officer, An Post; Graeme John, Managing Director, Australia Post; Georges Clermont QC, President and CEO, Canada Post; Hank Klassen, Vice-President/Administration, Canada Post; Ian Bourne, Senior Vice-President/Chief Financial Officer, Canada Post; Helge Israelsen, Chief Executive Officer, Denmark Post; Knud B. Pedersen, Deputy Chief Executive, Denmark Post; Dr. Klaus Zumwinkel, Chief Executive Officer, Deutsche Post AG; Richard Hochhauser, Executive Vice-President, Harte Hanks; Yves Cousquer, President, International Postal Corporation; Tan Sri Zainol Mahmood, Executive Chairman, Pos Malaysia; Gonzalo Alarcon Osorio, Director General, Servicio Postal Mexicano; Ad Scheepbouwer, President, PTT Post, Netherlands; Elmar Toime, Chief Executive Officer, New Zealand Post; Ulf Dahlsten, President and CEO, Sweden Post; Reginald Brack, Chairman, Time, Inc.; Marvin Runyon, United States Postmaster General and CEO, United

States Postal Service; Michael Coughlin, United States Deputy Postmaster General, United States Postal Service; William Henderson, Chief Operating Officer and Executive Vice-President, United States Postal Service; James Grubiak, Vice-President/International Business Unit, United States Postal Service; Allen Kane, Senior Vice-President and Chief Marketing Officer, United States Postal Service; John Roberts, Chief Executive, The Post Office, United Kingdom; Jerry Cope, Managing Director, Strategy and Personnel, The Post Office, United Kingdom; Kevin Williams, Managing Director, Parcelforce, United Kingdom; and Kumar Ranganathan, The World Bank.

We're extremely grateful to both Sir Leon Brittan and Thomas Leavey for their contributions as writers of this book's foreword and afterword, respectively.

Our gratitude also goes to the many other postal executives who helped shape our understanding of the transformation of this industry, and our colleagues, the professionals at Coopers & Lybrand who help us track and articulate the transformation of the postal industry. We would specifically like to thank consulting partners Joseph Kehoe, David Carr, Grady Means, and Robert Reeve; the members of the UK and US Postal Sector Client Service Teams; Pat Lafferty, of Coopers & Lybrand's Ottawa, Ontario, Canada office; Rosemary Radcliffe and Frank Milton, of Coopers & Lybrand's London, U.K. office; and Rogerio Casas-Alatriste, with Coopers & Lybrand in Mexico City, Mexico.

A special thanks is extended to the Coopers & Lybrand managers and staff who carried the burden of keeping us organized and productive, and who made this project a reality: Deborah Bowker, Paul Taffinder, Jane Angell, Christopher Melling, Matt Shinkman, Andy Paradis, Mike Clover, Karen Portman, Denise Clark, Susan Amy, Richard Batty, Melanie Williams and Patrick Scroggins.

Finally, we'd like to acknowledge the support of our editor E.J. Kahn III, and writers Michael McCullough and Carl Vigeland.

— John Dowson, Ed Horgan and Wood Parker.

# Foreword

## Postal Services as a Global Business

BY SIR LEON BRITTAN
VICE PRESIDENT, EUROPEAN COMMISSION

Despite major efforts to introduce market principles into large sections of the economy in the UK, the United States and throughout Western Europe since the early eighties, some key areas remain only partially open to market forces. These include areas traditionally seen as falling under the government umbrella, such as telecommunications, air or rail transport, and the gas or electricity markets.

The guiding principle of this tendency has been the realization that in most instances there is no contradiction between guaranteeing basic essential services for the public at reasonable prices and letting the private sector offer other services in a climate of free competition.

Postal services have proved to be among the most resistant to this process. They are still controlled by State monopolies in many countries, including most of the European Union's Member States. Those calling for greater competition within the EU often meet the following arguments: firstly, that without monopoly control of many profitable services, less profitable deliveries across the country as a whole will suffer. Secondly, that competition may lead to job losses among people with little chance of finding work elsewhere.

In addition, there is considerable resistance to change in organisations used to working in a heavily regulated and protected environment, while some postal operations have not been managed along business lines or have not been kept at arm's length from governments themselves.

It is this resistance, rather than the introduction of competition itself, which is jeopardising not only the provision of quality postal services to customers but also the survival of postal services as we know them. If public postal organisations oppose fundamental reform they will be unable to adapt to technological and market developments which currently threaten their very security. For instance, a letter may be delivered by fax within seconds from Frankfurt to Boston at the cost of a few pfennigs. If a text is sent by electronic mail it may take a few hours but could cost even less and can be edited on arrival. In addition, specialized companies can provide extremely efficient services for the delivery of printed and press matter — and so called direct mail — and whenever a guarantee of quick delivery for an urgent document is required, express delivery services leave traditional postal services trailing far behind.

Delivery times for letters are improving, but still only 77.6% of international mail within the EU arrives within three days of being posted and on average less than 90% of internal mail is delivered the day after postage.

In this rapidly changing environment, postal operators need to adjust to the more demanding needs of an increasingly international marketplace. They can no longer limit their business to the customary collection, sorting, transport and delivery of letters and other posted items. Conventional services are bound to decline in importance and added value compared to other activities. Now that the information society has broadened the use of personal computers linked up to each other through the internet or other future networks, postal organizations may need to plug into new technologies in order to provide higher value-added services such as postal delivery of letters generated by electronic mail and reproduced by the postal operator itself.

Postal organizations need to operate as profit-seeking businesses in competition with other entities. This will oblige them to carry out separate accounting of their different operations and services in order to improve their cost-efficiency, to develop new income-generating services, to be free to expand into other complementary areas and to organize themselves with the flexibility that any private company in a fast-moving services sector requires.

Insofar as national postal organisations are obliged to provide unprofitable services, certain mechanisms could be found to compensate for losses incurred. But this need not always be the case. Finnish and Swedish experiments at complete liberalization of postal services in large, low-density areas have proved that national postal bodies can outdo their competitors in some areas. Furthermore they are virtually the only profit-making postal organisations in the European Union, together with the Dutch - also liberalized - and the British systems.

Do national postal organizations need to be privatized? Theoretically, competition would oblige them to operate more efficiently even if they remain state-owned. In practical terms it would gear them up to competing in the marketplace in search of profit and therefore to providing better, more varied services to customers. Private status would ensure that they take businesslike decisions and operate under normal commercial terms without subsidies. It would also give them greater access to finance and enable them to enter new areas of related business such as finance, cash transmission and payment services.

Within the European Union it is largely up to national authorities, not the EU, to enact such a vision of the post as a dynamic, forward-looking service. The Treaty of Rome is explicitly neutral regarding the private or public ownership of any service or business, and the organisation and improvement of postal services are questions for the Member States themselves.

Yet through an active application of European competition policy in the postal sector, the Union can stimulate competition, innovation and greater respect for the customer.

With these objectives in mind, the Commission has published a draft notice on the application of competition rules to the postal sector. It indicates that items weighing under 350 grammes and priced at under five times the basic public tariff could be reserved for the monopoly. Up to the end of the year 2,000, incoming cross-border mail and direct mail could still be excluded from competition. Another draft directive under discussion in the Council and the European Parliament would involve further harmonization and quality standards for postal services.

If these drafts become law they would fall short of ending postal monopolies, but would nonetheless liberalize some 20% of the postal market (5% represented by incoming intra-EU cross-border mail and 15% by direct mail). However, these texts would have the important effect of enabling national postal bodies to perform like commercial companies in a competitive market.

Any delay in liberalizing postal services in the European Union would not only leave a gaping hole in the single European market, missing a chance to cut costs (losses represent up to one third of the revenue of some postal organisations), improve efficiency and benefit consumers. It would also hit national postal operators hardest of all, denying them the incentive to cope with technological change and meet the challenge of global postal and related services as they evolve. A rearguard action by monopolies to retain their grasp of basic services whose relative market value will decline anyway could stifle the energy and business acumen that postal operators so urgently need if they are to serve themselves and their customers properly into the next century.

*Sir Leon Brittan is Vice-President of the European Commission and has been a member since 1989. From 1989-92 he was responsible for Competition Policy and Financial Institutions. Since January 1993 he has been responsible for External Economic Affairs and Trade Policy. From January 1995 he has been responsible for Trade Policy and for bilateral relations with North America, Australia, Hong Kong, Japan and Korea.*

*Educated at Haberdashers' Aske's School, Cambridge and Yale, Sir Leon was called to the Bar in 1972, became a QC in 1978 and a bencher of the Inner Temple in 1983. He was knighted in 1989.*

*In 1974 he entered Parliament as Member for Cleveland and Whitby, holding various shadow posts. Following the general election in 1979, Sir Leon was appointed Minister of State at the Home Office. In 1981 he joined the Cabinet as Chief Secretary to the Treasury, became Home Secretary in 1984 and was Secretary of State for Trade and Industry from 1985 to 1986. In 1983, following boundary changes, Sir Leon was elected MP for Richmond, North Yorkshire, which he remained until he took up his present post in Brussels.*

*Sir Leon is now based in Brussels but frequently returns to London and North Yorkshire.*

# Chapter

# 1

## THE WORLD IS CHANGING

*No nation was ever ruined by trade.*
— Benjamin Franklin, first United States Postmaster General

One by one, the chief executives of the postal administrations in New Zealand, Australia, Sweden and Canada presented their testimony. One by one, they described — in compelling detail — how market and regulatory reform had driven their organizations towards greater efficiency, more profitability, increased innovation and better customer service. One by one, in the midst of the most bitter, snow-filled winter in the history of the capital of the United States of America, the directors of some of the world's most progressive posts painted a portrait of nothing less than an emerging global transformation.

In New Zealand, said New Zealand Post Limited Chief Executive Officer Elmar Toime, the postal administration had been named private corporation of the year in November 1994.

In Australia, noted Australia Post Managing Director Graeme John, financial performance had leapt from a break-even situation to revenues and profits that compared favorably with his country's most successful businesses.

In Sweden, postal President Ulf Dahlsten proclaimed, first-class deliveries were made overnight 96 percent of the time, despite a mandate to serve nine million citizens in "the last remaining wilderness of Europe."

And in Canada, observed Canada Post Corporation President and Chief Executive Officer Georges Clermont, all information technology development and property management had been outsourced, allowing his organization to concentrate on its core service — and in doing so, improve on-time delivery targets from 85 to better than 97 per cent.

None of these leaders suggested they were resting on these laurels. All emphasized they were engaged in

further substantial changes that kept them moving forward.

The two leaders of a United States Congressional
joint postal oversight panel — Ted Stevens, a Senator
from the country's northernmost state, Alaska, and John
McHugh, a Representative from a small inland city
more than 100 miles west of New York City — listened
intently. The last major reform of the United States
Postal Service had occurred in 1970, when then
Postmaster General Winton M. Blount convinced
President Richard Nixon to eliminate the postal administration as a government department, ending its tradi-
tion as a bastion of political patronage, and reconstruct
it as a quasi-independent agency operating under the
watchful eye of an appointed Board of Governors. At
the time, such change had seemed revolutionary. A
quarter century later, however, the structure seemed
cumbersome, inflexible and unresponsive in key areas
to the changing marketplace. Stevens, McHugh and
their colleagues seemed to understand the time for more
change had arrived. And that these changes were well
underway in Europe, in Asia and the Pacific, and in
South America.

But, now, as the scope of reform possibility was laid
before them, the two legislators kept their own counsel.
It would be six months before the United States took the
next small step towards market and regulatory reform.

The rest of the world, needless to say, wouldn't wait.

**The Global Environment**

The United States Postal Service is the world's
largest post — in revenues, in both quantity and variety
of mail handled daily, in number of employees, in scope
of operation. In *Postal Performance*, we will examine
many postal industry issues in the context of the United

States. Due to both its size and the scope of its business activities, the USPS undertakes innovative programs and initiatives in a range of areas. Many posts benchmark themselves against the USPS in these activities. But we will also highlight innovations in other posts in Europe, Asia and the Pacific, and North and South America, whose size offers agility and flexibility, and whose marketplaces are more liberalized.

In fact, the appearance of many of the world's postal leaders before the Congress of the United States underscored both the need, and the options available to further commercialize a post's operations. Greater degrees of transformation — to corporatize, giving management more flexibility, and to privatize by selling equity in a postal service to outside investors — were also displayed as a way to respond to the new global economy (though privatization, as a United States approach, seems almost unimaginably distant).

For both public and private sector organizations, global postal officials recognized, the nineties — following the expansionary 1980s — had brought a challenging business environment. There had been a prolonged slowdown in global economic growth as a number of key economies in the developed world slowed or went into outright recession. Growth in the Organization for Economic Cooperation and Development (OECD) countries averaged around one percent, compared with more than two-and-a-half percent growth through the 1980s. The slowdown had also been extended because the business cycles of the major economies had been on different timepaths. In North America and the United Kingdom, for example, where high levels of private sector indebtedness built up during the late 1980s, recession had come early and recovery had been sluggish, whereas in Japan, Germany and France the downturn came later and serious problems are still being experienced. The combination put industry and commerce worldwide under intense competitive pressures. And many businesses had to implement rigorous business reengineering and turnaround programs in order to survive.

Postal officials understood there was reason for optimism. The North American Free Trade Agreement (NAFTA) and GATT would provide a boost to world trade volumes, and OECD annual growth rates of around two percent were expected for most of the remainder of the decade.

But they also knew there was reason for concern. Customers had grown more sophisticated. There was increased demand for improved levels of service at lower real costs. The introduction of new communications technologies meant posts, at best, would have to evolve and adapt to the new market created by those technologies; at worst, postal services would be battered by substitute technologies. Postal management — and management processes — would have to respond by entering into and supporting alliances with customers and business partners. Finally, the industry's changes would make posts have to move more quickly and be willing to take risks.

Rising resource costs would put pressure on competitiveness and their governments would likely be grappling with the necessity to provide services to an aging population. These would have direct impacts on their social mandates. In the United States alone, the cost of providing free mail service for the blind was estimated at $60 million annually. In Australia, meeting community service obligations was a significant part of Australia Post's annual review. Similar obligations were being funded worldwide.

Against this background, postal executives realized, liberalization of trade and the emergence of global markets for business would continue as two key drivers of shifting economic power. In line with these changes, governments would face new challenges. So would the postal industry. Alliances, partnerships, meeting new customer needs, and effectively serving this global economy would drive much of the world's progressive posts' strategic thinking.

We have already seen posts starting out on their developmental paths. Some approaches have been more successful than others. In the Netherlands, KPN has acquired the global courier group TNT. The enlarged KPN group will offer services in 200 countries with its own operations in 47 countries, will carry more than two million items of freight each week, and be the largest time-sensitive courier and postal group in Europe. Such an acquisition demonstrates how aggressive postal administrations can be in the market if they are given the powers to do so. KPN is willing to move from the typical risk adverse approaches adopted in the past and the deal will position them as one of the few truly global postal administrations of the future.

Of course, government priorities will depend on particular national circumstances, but public sector restructuring, privatization of state industries and civil service reform will dominate the agenda in many economies, particularly in the emerging nations of eastern Europe and the developing world. Policies to promote employment and encourage flexibility in labor markets will be key in those economies seeking new sources of advantage as traditional industries decline.

In this new global economic environment, there is both risk and uncertainty — high levels of indebtedness in both the private and public sectors of many countries; the possibility of retreat into protectionism by major trading blocs; increasing volatility and uncertainty about exchange rates; the risk of political and social upheaval in parts of both the developed and developing world — as governments are motivated to improve efficiency in the economy. They're motivated to reduce the state role in the economy. And among the methods that they can employ to reduce the state role and improve efficiency is the transformation of the postal industry, which is — in most economies — the largest single employer.

What this has meant — and will continue to mean — for the global postal industry is that both market liberalization and competition are being introduced. And posts have to respond. The question is, How? In *Postal Performance*, we will demonstrate their need to first *commercialize*, and what that involves. From that transformation (see Figure 1-1), we will show how some posts have become *corporatized*. And still others — here the numbers are few, though the examples striking (and will undoubtedly grow) — have been *privatized*.

Figure 1-1

## The Transformation Path

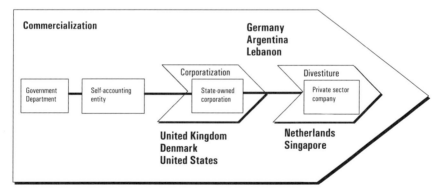

Gaining the powers to respond to liberalization and competition is the goal of this first commercialization phase. Management needs to be empowered (and needs the skills to exploit the empowerment), and the empowerment process typically gathers momentum from structural reform that moves a post to be more like a business. Further structural reform, we'll show, leads to corporatization and, eventually in some cases, to privatization.

But all are driven by the changing external environment.

## Lessons from Down Under

Against this background of global change, the world's postal leaders had gathered in Washington in January 1996. And the postal mountain was waiting for its Mohammeds.

The United States Postal Service, the world's largest, busiest and richest by a significant factor, had watched change from afar. In the Netherlands, in New Zealand, in Chile, in scores of smaller countries both on the U.S. borders and thousands of miles distant, postal administrators — freed from many of the restrictive regulations limiting the USPS's ability to introduce new products, new pricing, and new processes — had transformed their organizations into being more efficient, profitable and responsive to their customers.

The journey, the representatives of Australia, Sweden and Canada emphasized, had been neither smooth nor swift. In Australia, said Australia Post Managing Director Graeme John, the pace had been one of "steady change", a cultural transformation that had raised the post's financial performance from break-even to a profitability that rivaled that of the country's most successful businesses. Indeed, added John, profits from postal products and services had quadrupled since 1989.

The United States' Congressional leaders paid close attention as John reviewed the Australia Post's past two decades. His company — as documentation presented by John to committee members clearly showed — operates today in a highly competitive environment populated by both alternative service providers and substitute products based on advanced telecommunications. Under a mandate to provide national letter service, Australia Post nevertheless derives nearly 50 percent of its revenue from services open to competition.

Wholly owned by the government, Australia Post was established as the Australian Postal Commission in 1975. Fourteen years later, the passage of the Australian Postal Corporation Act continued the enterprise as the Australian Post Corporation. Providing letter and parcel services both domestically and internationally, the enterprise also offers a range of related services through its retail outlets. The services include bank deposits and withdrawals, utility payments, payments for telecommunications services, and passport processing. Because it is run as a commercial entity (and must abide by the same laws applicable to any other business), Australia Post turns a profit, pays all taxes, and returns annual dividends to its owners, the Australian government.

Australia's national letter service mandate, John explained in Washington, was universal and had to meet quality and performance standards, and uniform price restrictions. Consequently, some of that letter traffic operates at a loss. Those losses, legislators determined, met Australia Post's prescribed social and community service obligations. The losses, the government also decided, permitted Australia Post to retain a monopoly within certain price and weight limits. But even in monopoly situations, the post's losses — where they occurred — had to be subsidized internally.

An independent commission — the Australian Competition and Consumer Commission — reviews letter price proposals under the provisions of a Price Surveillance Act, John explained. Basic postage is capped under a formula tied directly to the consumer price index.

The numbers associated with the fiscal year ending in June 1995, added John, bore out the success of the Australia model: 31,600 full-time and 4500 part-time employees, 4300 post offices, 3.8 billion articles handled, $2.2 billion in assets, $2.8 billion in revenues, and a pre-tax profit of $331.6 million. Those revenues generated $245 million (in U.S. dollars) in taxes and government fees, and the profits delivered a $120 million dividend.

How had the Australian model evolved? Graeme John began by summarizing the post's history prior to the 1975 legislation. "Just a short time ago," he noted, "Australians were far less complimentary about their postal service."

Beginning in the mid-Sixties, concerns had been raised about the operation of the Postmaster General's Department of Government, known to most citizens as the Australian Post Office (APO), and responsible not only for mail but telecommunications as well. By 1975, a government report stated, "In the profit and loss sense, postal services have been a problem area within the APO for a number of years. Consistent losses have largely offset profits delivered from the telecommunications services." Indeed, Australian postal operations had experienced a decade of consecutive annual deficits. And performance levels were mediocre: although the percentage of on-time deliveries was in the high nineties in most states, the country's largest state, New South Wales, had never exceeded 90.5, and in some years had dropped as low as 75. Labor relations, during this time, had been colored by disputes and stoppages.

The need for reform, said the 1975 government inquiry (known publicly as the Vernon Report, after the chairman of the commission conducting the investigation), was driven equally by the problems with profitability, with performance, and with relations with the work force. In the New South Wales capital of Sydney, the Vernon Report observed, "the unsatisfactory industrial climate...evidenced by the number of stoppages and black bans, the frequency of meetings between management and staff and the difficulties of making changes in procedures, is unique." Nevertheless, concluded the report, it was "one of the major problems" facing Australian postal managers, and without a solution, the entire system was threatened.

## Australia's Phased Transformation

The answer to the Australian postal crisis came in four phases (see Figure 1-2).

The first happened later in 1975, when the bill creating the Australian Postal Commission passed. This act made the country's postal authority a separate entity from government. No longer a department, Australia Post had a new financial objective: to break even, and to provide, through its revenues, 50 per cent of its spending capital. After an early slump in volume, the financial performance was on target. But labor relations continued to be adversarial and, on occasion, disruptive.

By 1982, a new inquiry had recommended amending the letter monopoly, which was unlimited, to legalize private sector couriers. The couriers, growing in both numbers and business volume, hadn't been challenged by law enforcement anyway. The government agreed, reducing the price barrier to ten times the basic postage rate, liberalizing the market in the second phase of change there.

The third phase of reform, perhaps the farthest-reaching, took place in 1989, with the formation of the Australian Postal Corporation. Labor relations, said

John, "were at the breaking point", with both customers and businesses demonstrating little confidence in either postal service or management. That the government was willing to undertake such dramatic change, explained the Australian chief executive, was "an important incentive in encouraging the Post's management and unions to accommodate their differences, and led to the recognition of a shared interest — the continued viability and growth of the business."

The postal reform of 1989 fits into a "microeconomic agenda" of the Australian government, a determination that markets will work better if impediments

Figure 1-2

## Australia Post Transformation

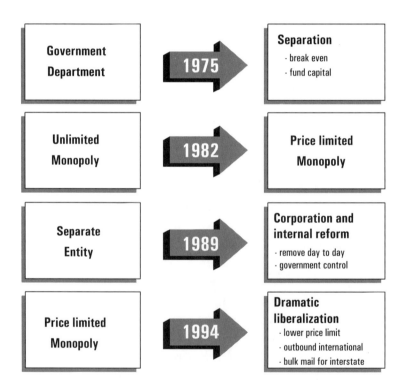

that discourage or prevent resources from being used in the most efficient manner are removed. Restrictions on competition, rigid work rules, and a distorted tax system were among those targeted by officials. Australia Post was one of several government business enterprises — many of which were assisted by a legislated monopoly — supplying goods and services, and most of which had felt the effects of deregulation, reduction of tariffs and other forms of protection, and introduction of competition.

The intent of the 1989 postal reforms was to corporatize the Australian Post, and through corporatization, to improve its efficiency. New corporate and financial structures were introduced, new planning and accountability mechanisms were put in place, major strategic controls were modified, and day-to-day control by the government was removed. Under the new relationship between the government and the post, the post would still meet defined social objectives, and would submit — every three years — a plan that included service, efficiency, pricing and profit targets, as well as projected community service objectives. Business taxes would be levied, and a dividend expected. "The government leveled the playing field," observed John. "All services must stand alone commercially; only the reserved letter service is internally cross-subsidized. All services are now subject to the competition reform legislation which applies to business."

The internal structure of Australia Post was transformed at the same time. A board of appointed directors would oversee its operations, and private sector executives would be recruited for top management roles. Tenure was abolished, and market-rate compensation for executives was put in place. Social objectives were differentiated from commercial ones, and Australia Post would — by law — from 1989 on have to achieve a "reasonable rate of return on assets."

A key to this more businesslike approach was the removal of day-to-day government controls. Contract oversight, land purchase approval and legislative review of major construction had all come under legislative authority. The 1989 act turned those activities over to the postal administration, along with the coordination of labor relations. With the charter of Australia Post transformed, leadership introduced performance measures and planning processes to push the changes throughout the organization.

"We've flattened management structures," John told the United States Congress, "removed job tenure for managers and reeducated them to focus on bottom-line outcomes, rather than bureaucratic empires. Autocratic management is a thing of the past. Because of the new relationship developed by labor and management, most of our people feel part of a team, proud of their achievements, proud of the commercial status and performance of Australia Post, and especially proud to work for one of the most successful Australian enterprises." With these changes came the ability for management to control the levers in running a business: pricing (within a regulatory or competitive environment), labor contracts and balance sheet funding.

Under corporatization, Graeme John, Australia Post interfaces with the government through two ministers: the Minister for Communications and the Arts, who is directly responsible for postal matters, and the Minister for Finance, who has oversight of the government's investments and assets. At the organizational level, the board of directors and management implement the strategic three-year plan agreed to by both parties. Pricing is left to the post, although the Minister of Communications can "disapprove" a proposal for the basic rate, if he or she chooses, and reserved services prices must be submitted for review by the Australian Competition and Consumer Commission.

There's little explicit financial protection for Australia Post, John noted. The post borrows in the open market, from the private sector, with government approval. It fully funds its employee pensions, and operates without cash subsidies. There is, John conceded, belief among financiers that an "implied" guarantee on the post's borrowings by the government does exist as a last resort. Whether or not that's the case, the Australia Post has considerable financial independence: it's free to buy and sell assets on a commercial basis (subject to restrictions on historic property and local development and zoning laws), and to make investments. Quarterly and annual performance reports are published, and each year the post must account explicitly how it met its community service obligations.

The independence extends to labor relations. While postal employees enjoy the right to strike (like any other worker in an Australian business), Australia Post is free to negotiate the outsourcing of any of its services or functions, after consultation with its staff and unions. Wages and work conditions are also subject to discussion with the government's labor department, before changes can be enacted. A Joint Statement of Understanding, agreed and signed by both management and labor in 1989, set out the process to guide future labor relations. This document, John told American legislators, allows "all people a say in decisions directly affecting their work."

Of all phases of reform, John said, none had more impact than the corporatization of 1989. After receiving a commercial charter and some distance from the government, the Australia Post achieved high levels of service performance, strong productivity growth and commercially credible levels of profitability. These have been accompanied by decreasing real postage prices, sustained mail volume growth, and substantial annual dividends. Also noteworthy was the "transparency" in planning, costing and delivery of the community service obligations that became embedded in the system.

This transformation's positive impact shines throughout almost every performance metric, John demonstrated (see Figures 1-4, 1-5 and 1-6).

Only once since 1976 — and never since 1989 — has Australia Post failed to record a profit. The price of a first-class stamp, adjusted for inflation and other factors, has fallen by a third in real currency since 1976. Mail volumes rose at annual rates usually higher than those of overall economic growth. Service quality, even with the introduction of an external audit in 1992, hov-

Figure 1-4

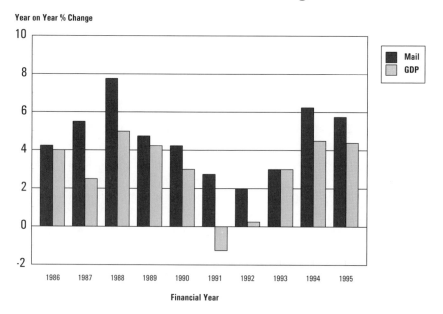

## Australia: Mail Volume and GDP
## 1985 to 1995
## Year on Year % Change

Figure 1-5

# Australia: Annual Labor Productivity Change % (Revenue at Constant Prices per Paid Workyear 1976/77 to 1994/95

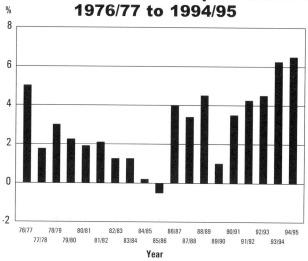

Source: Australia Post

Figure 1-6

# Australia: Corporate Annual Profit 1974/75 to 1994/95

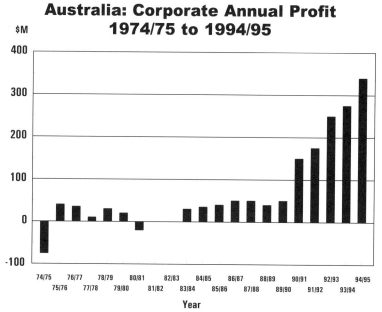

Source: Australia Post

ered above 90 percent. Productivity, profitability and the amount of the dividend paid back to the government all exceeded their historic highs in the year ending in June 1995. And time lost to labor disputes dropped to an all-time low of less than an hour per employee.

The final phase of reform — dramatic reduction in the scope of the letter monopoly (access to mail boxes had never been reserved for Australia Post) — began with wide-ranging industry commission inquiry and the subsequent enactment of the 1994 Australian Postal Corporation Amendment Act. This effort to transform the marketplace focused on three areas: the domestic letter monopoly, the international letter monopoly, and downstream access for reserved service. Protected letter monopoly prices were cut from ten times the basic letter rate to just four, and protected weights from 500 grams to 250. (On today's rate of 45 cents, that's $1.80.) Outbound international letter traffic was completely opened to competition (though not inbound). And bulk mailers were permitted to carry letters to designated mail centers for intrastate delivery only.

The letter monopoly, John's Washington documentation noted, had been modeled on that introduced to Britain by Rowland Hill in 1837. For more than 100 years, it mandated that only Australia Post could deliver letters weighing 500 grams or less. The first exception to that law was approved in 1982, when postal commissioners agreed that "urgent" letters could be carried by others, as long as the price was at least ten times the basic first-class rate, and the weight higher than the monopolistic maximum. A decade later, commissioners said they were ready to abolish the monopoly by 1995, but would compromise by progressively reducing its protection over a five-year span.

A further review will examine the remaining constraints on competition in 1997. "This 'steady change' formula," John said, "has been a major contributor to our success so far. We're better equipped than before to meet the challenges of our dynamic and contestable marketplace."

The legislators thanked Graeme John profusely. Change in the United States, too, they suggested, was on the way.

## Great Expectations

In the office tower over Washington's L'Enfant Plaza, United States Postmaster General Marvin Runyon had reviewed closely the testimony of his colleagues from Australia, Sweden, New Zealand and Canada. Their midwinter presentations had followed, by six months, a USPS-organized conference on the future of the global postal industry, a gathering that included representatives of several of the world's progressive postal administrations, as well as union leaders, executives of key customers and industry organizations, legislative staff members, top USPS executives and Board members. Much of the discussion had touched, both directly and obliquely, on the three fundamental differences between the U.S. Postal Service and the world's most progressive posts: that, in the United States, postal employees cannot strike, that all pricing is subject to lengthy rate commission review, and that mailbox access is reserved exclusively. For Runyon and his top managers, it was the beginning of the next step in their effort to promote change within and outside the U.S. Postal Service — a transformation, they believed, necessary for the USPS to compete.

Runyon had noted how Sweden Post president Ulf Dahlsten had offered reassurance that a liberalized marketplace would not lead to service degradation in rural areas. Swedish postal reform legislation, Dahlsten had said, mandated that the government ensure the service remain exceptional. "This gives the Swedish government an unlimited freedom," commented Dahlsten, "to contract (out to) any company on the market which is able to provide postal service."

Runyon had made note of New Zealand Post chief executive Elmar Toime's disclosure that his post's first-class stamp had dropped more than 30 per cent in real price since 1987, while the post itself had turned a profit every year.

Graeme John's remarkably constructive working relationship with his unions and employees had also been illuminating, Runyon thought. In July, at a symposium marking the 25th anniversary of the legislation establishing the USPS as an independent federal agency, Runyon would suggest that the size of his own work force — 874,982 men and women at the close of the 1995 fiscal year, more than any other non-military employer — was a significant impediment to becoming more businesslike. Being able to structure labor relations more like his colleague's in Australia, thought Runyon, would be a powerful first step.

And, from Canada Post Corporation president Georges Clermont, Runyon had noted Clermont's admonition that — following deregulation — Canada Post's concentration on operational improvements was a critical first step. "We had to give people a reason to believe in the system," Clermont had said. "It was important, first and foremost, to show Canadians that their postal system could do the job and give them good service. Having set standards of service, we had our performance measured by an independent auditing firm — we were the first to do so — and this allowed us to measure our progress, quarter by quarter, year by year." That, Clermont had said, became a key determinant for incentive awards to salaried employees.

All of them — Canada, New Zealand, Sweden and Australia — had assumed the postal industry leading-edge role played by the United States a quarter century earlier. Twenty-five years ago, the concept of alternative deliveries and substitute technologies — fax transmission, e-mails, overnight express services and the like — had eluded the framers of America's Postal Reorganization Act. To be competitive, flexible and customer-focused hadn't been a mandate, because the environment hadn't demanded it.

## The New Environment

Today, the environment is making demands. The growing convergence of telecommunications, computing and consumer electronics technologies was transforming the market for communications transactions. Driving much of the transformation of the postal industry is the emergence of new technologies, from the vast growth of the Internet to the development of new microchips. By one estimate, more than four of every five letters are now written on a computer, and in a growing number of cases the letter is then "mailed" electronically via networks such as the Internet. The ability of posts to retain market share against this kind of competition is fundamental.

So is the creativity of posts in finding uses for new technologies, both externally and internally. Many have already invested heavily in automation to increase productivity and make the mail flow more quickly and reliably. As new products become available, posts will not only have to adapt better but decide to do so faster.

A prime example is the Internet, where postal competition has for the most part been confined so far to e-mail. With the explosion of opportunities available through the World Wide Web, posts must now find ways to advertise and promote, distribute, and provide new products and services through this technology.

Virtually all western post counters are undergoing computerization, with the process taking many forms. The result is the elimination of much manual work and a tremendous increase in the scope of services. Australia Post, for example, has installed several thousand terminals in locations throughout its retail network. The United Kingdom's Post Office has also been computerizing its counters, with benefits coming in such areas as better customer/client cash processes. With a network of automatic cash dispensers, Belgium's post can compete with the banking sector, while the French postal system is going ahead with plans for a national electronic system that would permit payment of many bills at post offices and vending machines.

That's not to say that postal systems aren't facing intensive challenges raised by the implications of the technology explosion. "The postal system is thrashing around in a suit of barbed wire, attempting to be responsive to marketplace forces, and is restricted from doing that by a lot of very narrow self-interest groups that have constrained the pace of change," said Loren Smith, former Chief Marketing Officer for the USPS. "If this were a free-standing enterprise of this size, it would still have all the problems of being a big company, but it would be functioning very clearly against the things that are, in fact, impacting. One is marketplace forces. Two is the technology itself, which sometimes is a marketplace force, sometimes just a fundamental change in usage patterns of how people communicate. We are severely constrained by being responsive to two things that drive any enterprise — the marketplace forces and the technology that underpins the core industry. Those are the forces that are impacting us, and the government's in the way."

Allen Kane, who succeeded Smith as Chief Marketing Officer at USPS, believes the first priority is to focus on the basic business, "but there are other things that we've got to keep looking at because the world will change. Although we have a huge base of established businesses, you don't want to stay stand pat without looking for other opportunities. The problem you run into traditionally is the other opportunities become very controversial very fast. Invariably you get hung up trying to move through the controversy of doing non-traditional things, and then you forget about your established business. You can't forget where all the money is right now. The established businesses are your blocking backs, to use an American football term, and we should maximize what we can get out of them while — at the same time — keep looking for new products and new opportunities.

"If we have a game plan," says Kane, "there's always a way to make it work. In marketing, we need to explain the priorities and the 'why's' to the internal organization and external stakeholders. The funny thing about postal people is that if they understand where the mountain is, and they understand the path to the mountain, they'll take the path and get you to the mountain."

What the world's postal leaders had made clear in Washington early in 1996 was that their market had evolved, as had new technologies to help the posts — and their competition — improve service: optical character readers, bar code sorters, and remote bar coding systems. It was a lesson the USPS wanted to share. "We wanted to get on the table what people are doing in this world," said Runyon, explaining why the leaders had been invited to the United States capitol. "We were trying to make changes." Increased pricing flexibility, the ability to reorganize competitive businesses into deregulated, wholly-owned subsidiaries, and corporatization were of particular interest.

After the January presentations, Runyon — who'd earned his management credentials in the automobile manufacturing industry, first with Ford, then Nissan, and applied those lessons to the resuscitation of the Tennessee Valley Authority, a regional utility administration in the United States —- had gone on a fact-finding mission of his own, visiting Switzerland, Sweden, Finland, England and France. "I was impressed with what they do in post offices in Europe," Runyon recalled. "Some list job openings, sell bus and theater tickets, and have machines that accept credit cards. You could say they aren't just in the postal business; they're in the transportation and banking businesses, too. And you know what? That's the way you've got to do it, to meet the competition. You might have to go into a business that is very much your business, but doesn't look like your business."

To cite one example the Postal Service was already pursuing, Runyon described "Dinero Seguro" (or "Safe Money"), a joint venture with Bancomer, a commercial bank, and Servicio Postal Mexicano, Mexico's postal service, that will allow customers to electronically transmit — instead of by mail — money orders from United States post offices to branch banks or select post offices in Mexico. "Is that our business?" Runyon asked rhetorically. "Well, we've been selling money orders for more than a century. This is a new way to provide that service, and it's what our customers want."

Runyon's travels abroad convinced him as well that United States post offices have untapped retail potential, in part because their locations were never planned as a retail opportunity. "Post offices are often in inconvenient locations for a customer who wants to buy a postal product," said Runyon. "We need to put them in the right places, and we need to market and merchandise our postal products more efficiently. But we're doing that." In Pittsburgh, Pennsylvania, a new store in a central downtown location earns eight times the annual revenues of its predecessor. In Albuquerque, New Mexico, every post office has been transformed into a retail outlet. Not that the transformation has been perfected.

"We're not walking, we're crawling," conceded Runyon. "Our managers will put a $6 item next to a 15 cent item. It looks great, but the merchandising needs more professionalism."

Like his colleagues overseas, Runyon's focus remained on raising revenues, not rates. To accomplish that, he explained, he needed more flexibility and less oversight. "We've got Treasury oversight, Office of Personnel Management oversight, and Department of Transportation oversight," the United States Postmaster General commented. "I'm not sure the 1970 Act intended all that. We need the freedom to operate more like a private corporation."

Working within the existing oversight, Runyon said his priority would be to create "profit centers" — strategic business units, such as the one he has created to focus on the USPS's international business. "That's one of the reasons I went to Europe, and I'll be going to Japan and China soon, too. We need to set up partnerships with other posts. We have a package consignment service that can move a parcel from, say, L.L. Bean through Japanese customs and into the customer's hands in five days. That's comparable to our domestic service, and a six-fold improvement over our former service there. We're partnering with Japan now, not competing."

In a decade, suggested Runyon, the international business could grow from its current $1.5 billion in annual revenues to $10 billion. But the big picture, he added, is so often muddied by the small regulatory details. While global joint ventures may point the way to the future, a recent trip to upstate New York with legislator John McHugh underscored the constraints of the present. "I was there to introduce a new post card," said the U.S. Postmaster General, "and a reporter asked me where the next round of reforms might occur. 'We need a reclassification on service,' I responded, 'particularly on the post office box.' I explained that we had to petition the Postal Rate Commission to alter the price we charge for post office mail boxes, a process that can take two years. McHugh, who was listening to the exchange, was astonished.

"'You've got to go to the Commission to change the price on boxes?' he said. So I'm hopeful that any legislation will give us flexibility there, perhaps on a formula basis tied to the consumer price index."

Marvin Runyon, sitting under a five-foot tall portrait of Benjamin Franklin, the first Postmaster General of the United States, shrugged with some ambivalence.

"We've got to become competitive," he concluded. "Maybe we'll have to give up some of our monopoly. That's scary to our people. To me, too. But we've got to be competitive. So we've got to do what we've got to do."

## The Transformation

We listened intently to Marvin Runyon, and the scores of other postal executives, business leaders and senior regulators that we interviewed for *Postal Performance*. The industry portrait they painted — and that our research and decades of experience supported — was one of transformation, colored with uncertainty. The new competitive environment offered unprecedented opportunity to become more efficient and less costly. But it also created a very real possibility that the most profitable aspects of a post's business could be lost. We've drawn our knowledge from our personal experiences, our clients and from our annual CEO strategy forum, organized yearly since 1990. Collectively, we'd seen the impact of change from both inside postal organizations, and from the outside. John Dowson, working out of Coopers & Lybrand's United Kingdom headquarters in London, is one of the international postal industry's most experienced consultants, with clients on every continent. Ed Horgan is a former United States associate postmaster general. And Wood Parker is a Coopers & Lybrand Consulting partner based in Rosslyn, Virginia who leads the firm's relationship with the United States Postal Service.

Together, we understood the challenges facing both governments and posts: how to deliver services more efficiently; how to become more responsive to customers and taxpayers; how to reshape the postal sector into a powerful driver of an economy.

As we suggested earlier, this book will demonstrate how that transformation is taking place. In the chapters ahead, we will discuss the three phases of transformation —- *commercialization, corporatization,* and *privatization* — that organizations move through. We'll examine the external drivers pushing those phases, and the characteristics of change within an organization as it becomes commercialized, corporatized or privatized.

Marketplace change — the relaxation of constraints against competition and the amendment of the letter monopoly — will also be examined.

We will take an in-depth look at several posts we believe to be valuable case studies illuminating these phases of change. Australia and the United States, of course, we have already touched upon. Others will include Sweden, Germany, New Zealand, Argentina, Malaysia, Denmark, Canada and the United Kingdom.

And we'll conclude *Postal Performance* with an attempt to predict the future: where will this transformation move the industry in the next decade? We'll try to answer what we believe are the "big questions" that trouble and challenge postal sector leaders. In the end, the fundamental message for global posts seems to be, "Get commercial quickly." If the postal industry doesn't learn how to compete, its leaders will find themselves protecting a narrower and narrower monopoly to a business whose volumes are inevitably growing smaller.

### Forward...And Back

On Tuesday, June 25, 1996 — five months after the global postal presentations before the United States Congress — Representative McHugh unveiled his proposal, the Postal Reform Act of 1996, for the structural reform of the world's largest post. The McHugh plan called for a new relationship between the Postal Service and the Postal Rate Commission, with greater freedom extended to the Postal Service to set rates for its competitive services. Where services were covered by the letter monopoly, McHugh's legislation called for prices to be set under a price-cap regime that incorporated a gross domestic product index to keep rates within prescribed inflationary bounds.

The Postal Rate Commission would be directed, under the proposed bill, to determine an "adjustment factor" that could be applied over a five-year period to the agreed-upon price index for non-competitive services, and that determination would follow a rate case-like hearing.

The 1996 Postal Reform Act would require the United States Postal Service to operate profitably, and to use those profits for compensation bonuses, debt retirement and rate control. Experimental products and services could be introduced without Rate Commission approval, although such approval would have to follow within three years. Volume discounts could be offered. Letters would be redefined to permit private carriage for fees beginning at $2. Corporate titles would become the norm, with the board of governors becoming directors, and the postmaster general the chief executive officer. A "demonstration project" designed to test the feasibility of allowing non-postage items to be deposited in private mailboxes would start, and continue for three years. And the entire system could start after an 18-month final "baseline" rate case under current procedures had been conducted to provide an accurate starting point.

By Marvin Runyon's figuring, the bill could cost the United States Postal Service $2 billion in the reform's first year. Meanwhile, new revenues would be delayed for a year and a half by that last provision. "This imbalance between revenues and costs is a deep concern to us," Runyon told the American Congress two weeks after the legislation's announcement.

There were other problems, too, the Postmaster General pointed out. The international business unit, currently fully deregulated, would be re-regulated. Two additional layers of oversight — the Federal Trade Commission and the Department of Justice — would be added, and the Postal Rate Commission's authority would be expanded to a degree where it overlapped with the Postal Service's Board of Governors. Rate-setting could be further simplified, Runyon suggested. "We want to set pricing guidelines that are clear from the start," he said. "That everyone can see, anticipate, and budget for."

Finally, said Runyon, in giving the Postal Service more flexibility, the legislation would also add considerable costs: a billion-dollar debt obligation previously held by the government; $60 million annually to pay for free service for the blind; a worker's compensation obligation that could cost $240 million; and the risk of losing $4 billion in letter business to competitors taking advantage of the relaxation of the letter monopoly.

"Reform," concluded Marvin Runyon, "is a long process. We're going to be in it for the long haul."

The mail box debate could wait for another day.

| | Argentina (1995) | Australia (1995) | Canada (1995) | Denmark (1995) | France (1995) |
|---|---|---|---|---|---|
| 1995 GDP (US $ Billions) | 284 | 381 | 565 | 137 | 1,289 |
| 1994 Population (millions) | 34.2 | 18 | 29 | 5.2 | 58 |
| Area km$^2$ (000s) | 377 | 7,713 | 9,976 | 43 | 552 |
| Owner | Government | Government | Government | Government | Government |
| Date of last major reform | 1993 | 1989 | 1981 | 1995 | 1991 |
| 1995 stamp cost (US$) | 75 cents | 32 cents | 32 cents | 59 cents | 59 cents |
| Employees | 20,037 | 31,621 | 63,478 | 25,027 | 291,254 |
| Items handled (millions) Total | 444 | 3,827 | 11,800 | 2,662 | 23,624 |
| Domestic | N/A | 3,530 | N/A | 2,633 | 22,577 |
| International - out | N/A | 146 | N/A | N/A | 321 |
| International - in | N/A | 151 | N/A | N/A | 411 |
| Parcels | 0.5 | N/A | N/A | 29 | 315 |
| Post boxes | 10,431 | 13,000 | 87,368* | 11,000 | 136,500 |
| Revenue (US $ billions) | 0.45 | 2.15 | 3.6 | 1.5 | 16 |
| Profit (US $ millions) | (41.4) | 176 | 20 | 101 | (255) |
| Post Offices | | | | | |
| Most franchised? | Yes | Yes | No | No | No |
| Number of counters | 6,367 | 4,313 | 18,500 | 1,291 | 17,000 |
| Nature of retail services** | Wide | Wide | Basic | Wide | Wide |
| Pays income tax | Yes | Yes | Yes | Yes | Yes |
| Joint ventures | No | Yes | No | Yes | Yes |
| Subsidiaries | No | Yes | Yes | Yes | Yes |
| Financial Target | Break-even | Profit | Rate of return comparable to private sector | Profit | Accounting Equilibrium |
| Scope of monopoly | Liberalized market | 4x standard rate, up to 250g | 3x standard rate (30-50g) | Domestic letter post | Up to 1 kg |
| Monopoly obligations | Yes | Yes | Yes | Yes | Yes |
| Monopoly price cap | Yes | Yes RPI-X | Less than CPI | No | Yes |

\* Excludes rural and community collection points  \*\*\* Paying income tax beginning 1 January 1996
\*\* Wide—wide range of services offered
   Basic—government and post transaction only

| Germany (1995) | Malaysia (1995) | Netherlands (1995) | New Zealand (1995) | Sweden (1995) | UK (1995) | US (1995) |
|---|---|---|---|---|---|---|
| 1,903 | 87 | 316 | 61 | 221 | 1,043 | 7,254 |
| 81 | 20.7 | 15.4 | 3.5 | 8.8 | 58 | 261 |
| 356.8 | 330 | 40.8 | 266 | 449.9 | 244.1 | 9,373 |
| Government | Government | Government & private | Government | Government | Government | Government |
| 1995 | 1996 | 1994/95 | 1987 | 1994 | 1984 | 1971 |
| 61 cents | 12 cents | 43 cents | 27 cents | 52 cents | 41 cents | 32 cents |
| 341,910 | 11,914 | 36,000 | 9,284 | 46,048 | 191,300 | 874,982 |
| 20,674 | 1,076 | 6,100 | 939 | 4,373 | 17,488 | 184,060 |
| 19,073 | 914 | N/A | 868 | 4,210 | 16,751 | 180,700 |
| 1,005 | 106 | N/A | 40 | 93 | 717 | 800 |
| N/A | 55 | N/A | N/A | 26 | N/A | 719 |
| 596 | 1 | 40 | 31 | 44 | 20 | 1,841 |
| 140,000 | 53,415 | 18,500 | 146,000 | 38,000 | 120,000 | 283,000 |
| 18.7 | 0.2 | 3.4 | 0.42 | 3.1 | 9.2 | 54.3 |
| 237 | 11.5 | 258 | 69 | 107 | 490 | 1,770 |
| No | No | Yes | Yes | Yes | Yes | No |
| 17,000 | 1,496 | 2,200 | 4,553 | 1,875 | 19,603 | 39,149 |
| Basic | Wide | Wide | Wide | Wide | Wide | Basic |
| No*** | No | Yes | Yes | Yes | Yes | Yes |
| Yes | No | Yes | Yes | Yes | No | No |
| Yes | Associated Company | Yes | Yes | Yes | Yes | No |
| Profit | Profit | Profit | Profit | Profit | Profit | Break-even |
| up to 250 kg | Mail (All exclude courier) | up to 500g | up to US $0.52, 200g | No monopoly since 1993 | up to US $1.50 | 3x 1st class letter rate |
| Yes | Yes | Yes | Yes | Yes | Yes | Yes |
| Yes | Yes | Yes | Yes CPI-X | Yes | Yes | No |

*Sources:* UPU Postal Statistics 1994
Annual reports & accounts

# Chapter

# 2

## FROM LIBERALIZATION TO COMMERCIALIZATION

*"We have had to reinvent who we are and what we do, the kind of products that we develop, the kind of services. We have had to use technology in such a way that five years ago I would never have thought possible and we have had to ask fewer people to do more. I know every single one of you in the postal world is doing the same thing."*
— Reginald K. Brack, Chairman, Time Inc.

The clerk at the counter was polite but unhelpful. There was nothing she could do, she said. The package wasn't there.

"I don't know where it is," she said. "If I did, I could tell you when it will be here."

The customer was puzzled. The package he was waiting for had been mailed two days ago in the same state. It was traveling a distance of only 100 miles.

"How can it be lost?" he asked the clerk.

"It's not lost," she replied. "I just don't know where it is."

This answer seemed to the customer like the punchline to an ancient riddle. It was confounding, and extremely upsetting.

It was also extremely common. In this case, the incident had taken place in the United States, but it could have happened in any number of other countries.

There was a time, not so long ago, when such incidents were considered the normal way of doing postal business. It was no different than what happened in telecommunications or air transport. If a person experienced lousy service with the phone company there was nothing he or she could do about it. If a company wanted to make a deal for bulk express shipments, there was nothing it could do but continue to pay prices set through a government-sanctioned monopoly to a carrier licensed by that same monopoly.

Then the postal world began to change.

Throughout the world, governments are liberalizing their postal environments. Monopolies are being relaxed — both weights and prices of protected letters and packages are dropping dramatically. Competition is pushing its way through regulatory doorways expanded by a reduction in prohibitions against use of private carriers, in the spread of substitute technologies facilitating both communication and commerce, and in the dramatically higher expectations of both small and large customers.

As a consequence, the posts themselves have begun to change dramatically, too. In Australia, as we noted in Chapter One, the government has implemented partial liberalization of its market and given more commercial freedoms to Australia Post. The Canada Post Corporation, formed in 1981, has enabled that country's former post office department to make many improvements through commercialization of its operation. The Post Office in the United Kingdom has made great strides through the commercialization of its post, while in the Netherlands privatization has heralded a transformation.

Posts are using technology to enhance and extend their service portfolio. In Ireland, An Post has built advanced technological capabilities by itself and through joint ventures, and has started to market them worldwide. PostGEM, an An Post subsidiary, operates Ireland's largest managed communications network and provides Internet services. Through Infonet Services Corporation, an affiliate, PostGEM offers its customers access to over 170 countries worldwide. An Post is also part of the Pathway consortium led by ICL, an enterprise that has won a substantial contract for the computerization of the United Kingdom's Post Office retail network, including back office systems for the UK's national Benefits Agency.

Seen as a whole, these activities lead to one inevitable conclusion: a global transformation is underway as posts become much more businesslike through commercialization. As Kumar Ranganathan, The World Bank's executive in charge of the postal sector, has said, "In several countries, the postal sector is at a critical juncture. If nothing is done and the status quo is maintained, then it is likely that the sector will continue to erode as competitors and other communications media take over the market."

## The Stages of Structural Transformation

As we shall examine throughout this book, as many as three stages are involved in the transformation of a post. The first is commercialization, or pushing a government department towards the behavior of a private enterprise in a competitive environment. The second is corporatization, where the enterprise's management is freed from government oversight to make day-to-day operational decisions relating to pricing, labor, product and service development, and infrastructure investment. The third stage is privatization, in which the corporatized entity expands ownership control through shares sold to private individuals and institutions, even to another public enterprise.

In subsequent chapters, this book will look at transformational stages of change in significant detail for a number of different countries that have achieved success. *Postal Performance* will also introduce a unique model for an organization's internal transformation: *the corporate transformation wheel*, a proprietary framework developed by Coopers & Lybrand for understanding and promoting change within an organization trying to meet the challenges of a competitive business environment. In Chapter Nine, we will explain how this model's methodology is applied so an organization may become more effective, productive and closer to its customers. In this chapter, however, we shall limit ourselves to discussing the first phase of structural transformation, called commercialization. And because many governments have found that managers respond well to the partial liberalization of the market and to threat of further liberalization (and that customer benefits force these changes), we will also look at the evolution of competition.

Commercialization focuses on the adoption of private sector management techniques — improving revenues through participation in new product development, a focus on customer requirements, better quality, and greater efficiency. It assumes that the management authority, and its relationship to its government owners, remains essentially unchanged. But it also reflects the consequence of government recognition of a need for change. It must empower management to make change, and it can only go so far when a postal service is part of the government.

When management has exhausted the possibilities within government's direct control, it will often move that post to an arm's-length company still wholly owned by the government. This next step in structural transformation is known as corporatization. At this point the company is typically empowered to move outside government contractual requirements in such areas as labor negotiations and procurement. When a postal service corporatizes its operation, it is no longer a department of a government, but it is still state-owned. As an independently administered entity, it empowers a group of officers who can respond quickly to the needs of its customers.

While there are a number of state-owned posts in the world — notably Sweden, Germany, Denmark, Australia, New Zealand, South Africa, Malaysia, Argentina and the United Kingdom — the only fully privatized postal service at this time is the Netherlands. Singapore Post, however, has a substantial number of shareholders — not a majority — as a subsidiary of Singapore Telecom. Governments in countries where progressive change has been taking place are usually those that have also initiated market reform. By lessening the control of previous postal monopolies, customers typically enjoy improved service and greater choice of service. Alas, such regulatory bodies as the European Commission and the Universal Postal Union have been less progressive in creating a climate in which other countries might quickly follow the lead of those whose postal services have been commercialized. But there are positive signs this is changing.

## Changing Everything

Commercialization means changes. Changes in the marketplace drive changes in the way governments work, and governmental operations, in turn, drive changes in the postal sector. Domestically, competition exerts pressure to bring prices down which in turn puts pressure on the postal cost structure. To support this cost reduction and ensure a flexible distribution and marketing scheme, many administrations are looking for increased revenue from mail services, in addition to developing their counters networks and other channels and introducing improvements which change the process by which the postal business is managed.

"We've changed the way we do just about everything, and we're constantly seeking new ways," says Time, Inc.'s chairman, Reginald Brack, whose company is one of the largest customers of the United States Postal Service.

"Because there are competing media, the postal service has to get more private-sector like," declares Richard Hochhauser, president of Harte Hanks Direct Mail Services. "Time is measured differently in today's world," he continues. "People talk in soundbites and nanoseconds and quickstuff, and if you play in those arenas you find things moving very quickly."

In a triumph of logistics and implementation, as American Express vice president for corporate affairs Laurel Kamen points out, her company in a joint venture with the USPS was able to develop and market a new product — the first-class phone card — from start to finish in only 88 days.

"Companies are going global," points out James Grubiak, vice president of the United States Postal Service's International Business Unit. To Grubiak, as posts continue to commercialize, perhaps the key element is the collaboration that results from competition. For example, he cites "the bundling of services that will link into a customer's market timing — a customer's ability or need to send an advertisement, say, and get a response, or a package and get a remittance."

The overriding imperative for any postal service that wishes to survive as anything more than a supplier of last resort is to run a business that can evolve smoothly and quickly, and exceed the service expectations of its customers. This requires management talent, a cash flow-generating and profitmaking core business, an educated and flexible workforce, and an enlightened government.

## Marketplace Reform

### Customer Instigated

Advances in telecommunication, computing and media technologies are causing demand for communications transactions to grow in volume and sophistication. Postal businesses are growing ever smaller in their contribution to the overall communications market and need to learn new tricks. A preoccupation with protecting the postal letters monopoly only makes sense if it provides a limited period of time to give management the capacity to change the business. The environment is changing at such a pace that if postal businesses stagnate (as many still are) they will find that in ten years time their customers will have moved substantial volumes of transactions to other systems or processes.

Key customers (those providing large volumes of mail) are also finding their own businesses are changing quickly. They need a flexible postal service as a partner in their own change programs - a postal service which can also work in partnership with their other suppliers. The traditional introspective procedure- and operations-oriented postal service must become a thing of the past.

### *Government Instigated*

Governments have been changing the regulations around postal markets for many years.

A postal counters network is usually restricted in the range of products it can provide so as to protect the evolution of other private sector retail chains from a potentially dominant player in the community. After all, postal retail chains are almost invariably the largest and most dispersed in the economy. The retail network is further constrained by the regulations in the financial services industry which are designed partly to protect retail bankers and partly to ensure that more complex products are sold by properly qualified and trained staff.

Postal parcels businesses generally operate in a fully competitive environment yet maintain a universal service obligation (to provide a universal service at an affordable rate) so as to protect smaller businesses and the general public. Parcels businesses compete against a range of specialists which, on a small scale, can generate superior profits. They also fight against the largest integrators (eg. UPS or Federal Express) with their high quality of service and incorporation of high technology.

The letters business still enjoys monopoly protection in most countries in return for its universal service obligation. The nature of the monopoly varies widely. The US environment, for instance, is both highly and unusually constrained in restricting access to a customer's mail box and, at the same time, progressive in allowing for widespread access to the network as far as the delivery office.

The evolution of competition in the letters market will be an important driver of the commercialization of the postal operator. Governments that signal a progressive relaxation of the monopoly (as they did in Australia and New Zealand) have found that the postal service responds with rapid commercialization provided that the government is also prepared to mandate the management to get on with change.

However, some postal services are slower than others at being able to change (for internal reasons or, sometimes, because their political masters will not sanction change). Nowhere is this more evident than in Europe where special interest groups (which change over time) have been able to block progress towards a more liberal and harmonized European regulatory environment. The confused multiplicity of national positions has been further complicated by disagreements within directorates of the European Commission on how to move forward. Customers, competitors and progressive postal operators are both bemused and frustrated by this lack of progress.

"Judging by their actions," suggests Republic of Ireland's An Post Chief Executive John Hynes, "the group of 'public service' posts in Europe seem to be determined to avoid adjusting to market realities and they wish to enlist the European Union in this fruitless endeavor. Their actions have the potential to destroy postal solidarity by forcing the 'liberal and pragmatic' group of posts to pursue sensible reforms through market actions rather than through EU legislation."

And yet radical changes are coming through.

## Liberalization in Sweden and Finland

Notwithstanding the many different political, social, and economic circumstances that characterize different countries, all posts are experiencing increasingly aggressive competition and market liberalization. However, there are distinctive, regional changes taking place. For example, Sweden has eliminated the monopoly on letter distribution. This occurred in 1993, making Sweden one of the first countries in the world to achieve this landmark change in its postal service. As a monopoly, Sweden Post's public image had a detrimental impact on customer relations. The elimination of the postal monopoly in Sweden — supported enthusiastically by Sweden Post management and the Swedish public — greatly enhanced that image. The elimination of the postal monopoly led to increased competition (although this rise started slowly) and has stimulated greater effectiveness and efficiency within Swedish Post.

Sweden's Postal Services Act invoked on March 1, 1994 placed basic regulations on the postal market. Unlike so many other nations' postal laws, the Postal Services Act applied not only to the public operator but to the entire postal market including any private postal operations. These regulations were designed to protect and ensure access to postal services throughout Sweden. Under the act, the executive branch of government is responsible for ensuring there is a good postal service within the country. This means it may contract with any operator — public or private — to provide postal service.

"The basic question faced here," according to Sweden Post's Ulf Dahlsten, "is whether the postal service is a part of the market economy where consumer demands are governing, or whether it should be looked upon as part of a country's infrastructure, like highways. To me the answer is simple. To 95 percent, the posts are part of the market economy and should be run accordingly." Both Sweden Post and its competitors have found the evolution of the market difficult. Since liberalization, the Swedish Competition Authority has intervened a number of times to protect customer and competitor interests. The main competitor, City Mail, has had a particularly difficult time in managing expansion and trying to survive while senior management time has been directed towards litigation and regulatory debate. This competitive evolution is of great interest to the whole postal world because of the market dynamics, the political policy environment, the presence of a forceful competition authority, outspoken press comment and through detailed local academic interest. That is exactly what has been happening to the post in one of Sweden's neighbors, Finland, though the process is far from complete.

Finnish licensing rules for competitors have made for a restrictive environment in a so-called liberalized period. The new postal act in Finland, which took effect at the beginning of 1994, separated postal services and postal regulation. The Post of Finland became a limited company fully owned by the state and a new regulatory office — the postal administration — was established.

The Finnish postal administration, which became part of the telecommunications administration center, is responsible for supervising compliance with the act on postal services and other provisions issued thereunder. The postal administration is also the authority dealing with complaints concerning delivery terms and mail distribution. In practice, this means that the postal administration is an impartial authority involved in settling disputes between the postal operator and its customers. The postal administration is in close cooperation with the ministry of transport and communications, which deals with matters concerning postal policy, operating licenses and development of postal law and related provisions.

The Finnish Post has faced competition, at least on a limited scale, for several years already. Until 1991 the post had an exclusive right to convey "personal messages against payment." In practice there already existed open competition, even in letter business. The monopoly was formally abolished in 1991 and the post has been able, since 1992, to set independently all its tariffs and prices. Since then, the post has undergone considerable change for both increased efficiency and cost reductions in order to survive. The change seems to be a successful one and Finland Post Ltd. is today a profit-making company, although there is almost continuously ongoing public discussion blaming the post for reductions in the number of post offices.

Part of the reason for Finland's success is the careful manner in which the postal laws were reformed. According to the Act on Postal Services the operating licenses shall be granted if the applicant "is well-established and evidently capable of regularly providing postal services."

For the time being, the ministers have not been able to solve the problem of whether the new postal operator in the Helsinki capital area will affect the availability of postal services and the fairness of costs for sparsely populated regions or not. The solution to this problem will be of crucial importance for the future postal policy in Finland as well as for the development of the postal administration.

## Diversifying Service and Products

As markets are reformed, posts react by diversifying both product and service lines. Direct mail, flexible delivery, late collections, work sharing, and new payment mechanisms are all aspects of the diversification of posts' letters business in liberalized markets. In the parcels business, some posts now offer customers track-and-trace technologies, overnight delivery, and — for catalogue and other home-shopping services — warehousing and fulfillment.

Posts have been working with customers to assist in the development of the direct mail market. In almost every country, the level of direct mail per capita is increasing, and direct mail volumes have been a significant contribution to mail growth over the last few years. In the United States, the USPS has worked with customers to develop their campaigns. In other countries, discounts have been given to the volume direct mailers. Everywhere, postal authorities are involved in the development of comprehensive address and information databases which assist in the targeting of direct mail.

Sophisticated targeting of the mail receiver increases the hit rate/success rate of a direct mail piece, and senders traditionally have focused on high income/time constrained individuals. But — direct mailers now realize — a future opportunity may be the lower income individual who may be interested in credit deals associated with home shopping.

Whatever the opportunity, postal executives see it as real. As Royal Mail's marketing director, Jim Cotton-Betteridge, believes, "...there will always be a paper shell around the electronic media and while we may be losing market share of the communications market, we expect to see the postal market continue to grow."

A successful direct mail piece is one that produces a result, and generates mail in all other categories. It is the engine that drives volume in all other classes. For example, for a weekly magazine, you can mail at the very least 52 issues (there may also be some special issues). In the United States, these will be mailed as second class (recently changed to "Standard Class") and will generate perhaps four bills. By one estimate, when you add up the result of that one successful sale through a direct mail piece, including each edition of the magazine, there are at least 70 other pieces of mail volume forthcoming. And that is before you use the same household as a prospect for other kinds of goods and services sold and developed and marketed by the same company, in addition to other direct mail advertisers and marketers that use that same prospect.

In the future, posts will wish to expand direct mail through constantly improving the success rate per mail shot. This will require ever more sophistication in the uses of database applications and in market research. These are two more areas where alliances may be desirable.

Flexible delivery is another focus of diversification in liberalized markets. Customers of posts want to move to delivery on demand, and business mailers of value propositions or goods want to ensure that the receiver is in. Fully flexible delivery has to be balanced with costs, and niche competitors offer delivery options that are far more attractive than those offered by posts. But the posts are recognizing the need; Denmark is already offering evening deliveries.

The flexibility will eventually extend to late collection of mail, because of operational improvements. So too will it encompass work sharing — the introduction of team working arrangements under which the workforce is empowered to resolve operating issues as they think appropriate. Already introduced in the United Kingdom (where it's being challenged by organized labor's leadership) and Denmark, work sharing should increase employee satisfaction and improve customer service.

Finally, liberalized markets lead to new payment mechanisms: credit cards at the counters, and easier-to-use meters and invoicing for bulk mail. Gone will be the days of stamps as the sole retail option, and complex franking machines in office environments. Liberalization demands ease of access for both services and payment.

The parcel business is also transformed by liberalization. Postal competitors have had track and trace, for instance, for many years. Several — Federal Express and United Parcel Service, to cite two — are offering on-line access to big customers direct, and to any customer via the Internet. But posts are developing more sophisticated systems for national tracking themselves, and are integrating their systems for international tracking. In the home-shopping business, the anticipated growth rate (and attendant customer need for delivery) is driving posts to move up their customers' value chains to offer such services as warehousing and fulfillment, and the logistics to guarantee time-certain delivery. Overnight parcel delivery, another emerging customer need, is requiring posts to negotiate alliances with transportation companies — a relationship that has to be carefully managed to ensure a consistent service.

### Taking Advantage of New Technologies

In 1995, more letters were sent via e-mail in the United States than via the post office, according to a recent article in Forbes Magazine. As the United States Postal Service's Chief Operating Officer, William

Henderson, notes, "Where do you take that? How does a USPS deal with that emerging technology?"

For the USPS and posts in many other countries, the introduction of new technology from the telecommunications industry is forcing changes in the way posts operate. Increasingly, simply offering the traditional paper mail services to customers will not suffice, as vastly more efficient forms of sending messages and transactions electronically are offered by telecommunications companies. Recognizing this, postal leaders hope the United States government may some day allow the postal system more freedom to run itself like a private business. This will in turn allow the United States Postal Service not only to compete with the other options customers have for mail delivery, but may actually enable it to offer the new technology or products themselves or form alliances with other telecommunications businesses.

"The USPS, which is the biggest postal administration in the world, is trying to become more businesslike," says the United States Postal Service's Deputy Postmaster General, Michael Coughlin. But, as Postmaster General Marvin Runyon knows, "Once you do that...you're maybe at arm's length from the government, but you're still more or less influenced or regulated by the government."

Technology has forced this reform of posts in several ways (see Figure 2-1). Fax machines — and electronic mail — have replaced much of the market for paper mail services. They are faster, more efficient, and often less expensive. Yet technology is not necessarily a threat to the postal system. While it offers competition and an opportunity for a post to fall even further behind than it already has, technology also allows postal administrations to catch up, either by implementing new technology to enhance performance and productivity or by offering new technology driven products and services. Working more interactively with the telecommunications companies that already have the technology is another alternative.

There are several purely electronic services that posts are beginning to offer which have traditionally been offered by telecommunications companies. Electronic mail, or e-mail, in which text is sent directly from one computer to another over a connecting network, is probably the most well known. A post could provide the network, something which is done now by independent companies such as America Online and CompuServe. Another service which posts are starting to provide is electronic data interchange, which allows the transfer of data in a predefined structure, usually in the supply chain (order, dispatch and invoice). This can provide a substitute for paper order forms, invoices, and payments slips. Electronic funds transfer is yet another electronic service that can be offered by postal administrations. The electronic transfer of funds is replacing the use of cash in many areas of the financial services and retail industries. Technologies to support this include debit cards, where money is actually subtracted from a customer's account, and smart cards, where funds are stored electronically on the card itself. As paper mail continues to decline as a means of communications and doing business, it is crucial that posts offer such technologies. Posts need to make technologies such as EDI and EFT part of their value-added and/or new product service offerings in concert with using technology to improve, expedite and drive down costs in traditional mailing operations.

There are hybrid mail services as well that can generate added business for posts. Hybrid electronic mail is where a sender sends a message, perhaps to multiple addresses, in electronic format (over the telecommunications infrastructure) which can be printed, processed and formatted by the post for delivery to the requested address. Hybrid EDI allows business customers to provide EDI electronic data which the postal service can then print and deliver, fax, or send via a courier. A number of posts have begun to offer international fax, in which the fax is electronically routed to receiving stations in the postal system, where they are printed, enveloped, and delivered. Reply cards have also been introduced. The concept of the reply card is that it sends notification that "the check is in the mail." This service uses bar codes on the bill payment or remittance slips to inform firms electronically that the letter had entered the automatic mail stream.

Many Western posts' retail counters are undergoing computerization, with a variety of outcomes. One result has been the elimination of considerable manual work. Another is an increase in the scope of services. Australia Post, for example, has installed several thousand terminals in locations throughout its retail network. Great Britain's Post Office has also been computerizing its counters, with benefits coming in such areas as better customer-payment procedures. With a network of automatic cash dispensers, Belgium's post can compete with the banking sector, while the French postal system is going ahead with plans for a national electronic system that would permit payment of many bills at post offices and vending machines.

We shall look at technological change further when we examine the second state of transformation called corporatization.

## Solutions for Success

Diversifying products and services through market orientation and embracing technology are only two of the ingredients for success.

Postal services are typically the largest remaining civilian employer in most economies. Perhaps the biggest challenge is in motivation, training and cultural change at all levels of the organization - a daunting task within a state-directed environment and one which provides the most compelling reason to take the step of corporatization. The reskilling (including hiring of new skills) and changes to working practices aided by the introduction of new pay and benefits arrangements take three-to-five years and provide exciting results.

A further task is to ensure that government procurement roles do not build inefficiencies into a postal offering. We have observed historic examples of postal services being forced to buy international cargo space on a national flag airline at very high prices rather than going to the lowest cost provider for the required level of service. This kind of problem still exists in many countries, but if a government truly requires a commercialized postal operator, it must not compel the operator to subsidize other inefficient government activities.

A post can only do so much while it is a government-owned department. Then it hits barriers that can be removed only by corporatization. There are no real barriers at the level of corporatization. But if the government is unwilling to yield control over the balance sheet to a state-owned company, then divestiture may well be the ultimate solution from the aspect of management effectiveness.

The issue for the private sector is really one of competing on level terms with a state-owned company. A private company is always worried about joint ventures and risks that the state-owned companies enter into because it will say that whatever happens the post will not go bankrupt.

For commercialization to be successful therefore, the government needs to work in partnership with management. Management needs to make the business more responsive to its environment. Eventually, there comes a point when management hits barriers that could be removed by the corporatization step. But there is much that management can do by way of commercialization before a post corporatizes:

- It can go after cost reductions;
- It can go after efficiency and quality improvement;
- It can learn more about, and experiment in, market segmentation.

The issue, finally, is whether the government will allow this. Are there rules that are in place that the government has set, for whatever reason, which prevent the post from going as far as it can in revenue, cost reduction, efficiency, quality, procurement rules or labor negotiations?

As Marvin Runyon suggests, it may not be able to go as far as it wants to, in the face of government restriction. The step of corporatization moves a post to arm's length from the government and empowers it to adopt new policies, new management techniques, and new pay arrangements to recruit new senior people. That enables a post then to take some more steps along the corporatization path. But the fact that it does not have power to do that should not prevent it from taking the first steps.

New Zealand and Australia have gone through the whole cycle with overlaps between commercialization and corporatization. Denmark over the last 15 years has had a particularly interesting history. The post corporatized there in January of 1995, and most of its transformational change happened before corporatization. By embarking now upon a big technology-based change, it will completely alter its position in the market and pioneer a new position in its structural transformation.

As others follow suit, the postal industry will continue to transform itself into a more businesslike model.

# Chapter

# 3

## INTERNAL TRANSFORMATION—BECOMING MORE LIKE BUSINESSES

*"Postal employees are the lowest paid, but one of the most respected public servants. There is hardly ever a complaint from our customers."*
— Gonzalo Alarcon, Secretary General, Servicio Postal Mexicano

In the fall of 1995, United States Postmaster General and CEO Marvin Runyon walked into a meeting with the Postal Service's Board of Governors, and — brandishing data indicating a record revenue surplus (see Figure 3-1), rising volume, and improved local delivery times — told the Governors, "We have no intention of resting on our laurels."

Figure 3-1

## United States: Postal Profits and Losses

By fiscal year in billions

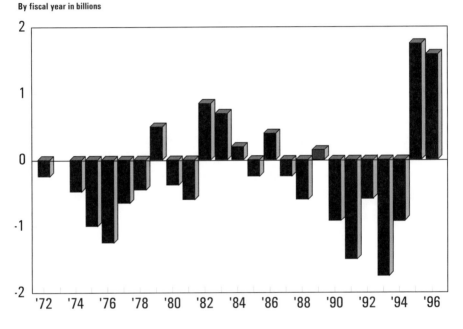

That Marvin Runyon and his management team would have laurels to rest upon might have surprised outside observers, and no small number of insiders as well, a year earlier. The USPS, they knew, had come under withering critical attacks in Chicago and Washington beginning in the fall of 1993. When the Postmaster General himself had flown to the Midwest to meet with some of the Illinois city's largest mail customers, he'd experienced the discontent firsthand. "Many of our customers were literally irate," recalled United States Postal Service Chief Operating Officer William Henderson. The complaints had been loudest in that nation's capital. There, the media, in particular the *Washington Post*, had spent much of the year chastising postal officials for poor delivery and service in the Washington Metro region, which extends into southern Maryland and northern Virginia. The criticism had carried into the United States Congress, where elected officials launched tirades against late letters, abandoned mail, and overdue packages.

Critics could point with justification to some of the Postal Service's own studies: in the Maryland suburbs, a 1994 survey had indicated, three-quarters of a batch of "test" letters had been delivered the day after they were mailed. The service had hoped for at least eight out of ten. In the District of Columbia, the score had been 71 percent; in northern Virginia, 73 percent. None of the USPS's ten national regions scored lower.

What most postal critics hadn't realized was that change was already underway. The Postmaster General, concerned with an organizational hierarchy that fostered turf consciousness and deferred accountability, had begun an initiative to streamline the structure. Instead of three corporate line managers, there'd be just one: William Henderson was named Chief Operating Officer. At the district level, plant and district managers would report to an area vice-president. "The Postmaster General," said Henderson, "thought there hadn't been enough field accountability. He wanted to drive quality. With this organization, the Postal Service became more focused at both headquarters, and in the field." Ten area vice-presidents, under the reorganization, would report directly to Henderson. No message from the field, under the new system, would get filtered at the top, and no myriad of disjointed messages would distract the field from service to its customers.

The reorganization, the increased attention to improved processes and better customer service were all elements of an effort on the part of the United States Postal Service to operate in a more businesslike manner. The Americans, like the Australians, New Zealanders, British, French and Chileans (to just name a few) before them, committed to commercializing their enterprise — a series of programs and initiatives senior officers felt imperative in order to compete against both emerging technologies, and expedited delivery competitors.

"The degree of competition is incredible," said United States Deputy Postmaster General Michael Coughlin. "Our people still do not fully appreciate how big it is. Part of that is because it's masked by continuing small growth in absolute volumes. They are continuing to tell themselves everything is all right, even though the rate of growth is about a third smaller over the last eight years than it had been the previous ten." The concern, Coughlin seemed to be saying, was that technology might not be driving greater volume, contradicting what many others believed.

### The Aspects of Internal Transformation

Internal transformation is part of the process of commercialization. If a government agency, department or independent (but wholly-owned) company is going to commercialize, it becomes incumbent on the organization to get closer to its customers. One cannot commercialize successfully without having a customer excellence program that includes customer measurements, linked rewards and recognitions, and an enhanced sense of employee empowerment.

Organizational initiatives designed to make enterprises leaner in order to face up to competition, and programs to maintain critical volumes while sustaining an acceptable level of tariff in the broader sense, must be launched by executives. Otherwise the enterprises risk loss of market share and declining profitability.

As we review the examples of internal transformation in the global postal industry over the past decade, we can identify several recurring initiatives or programs:

- Process reengineering — which may incorporate a management reorganization that "flattens" hierarchical levels, and improves communication throughout the company.
- Accountability through performance measurement — including the introduction of quality measures, and compensation/reward systems tied to those measures.
- Increased customer focus — including the introduction of technologies that allow for tracking and sorting of documents.
- Introduction of subsidiary enterprises, with independent accounting, management and distribution functions.

Most of these activities are, in fact, elements of a Coopers & Lybrand-designed approach we term *corporate transformation.* We'll examine it in detail in Chapter Nine.

In terms of corporate transformation implementation, France is an excellent example of the introduction of subsidiary enterprises. There, La Poste — which became an independent public company on January 1, 1991 — has developed three types of subsidiaries. First are enterprises offering high-quality products and services that enrich and complement those of La Poste itself, such as Chronopost and Tat Express, both of which offer express and/or expedited delivery services, and Mediapost — a direct mail provider that now runs the advertising activities of La Poste itself.

Second are companies which improve the operation and daily performance of the post's infrastructure and some postal services by offering cost reduction, quality, reliability or expertise: Aeropostale, a partnership with Air France and others to improve airmail transport (the organization introduced a quick-change system for Boeing 737s, permitting a switch from a nighttime cargo configuration to daytime passenger carrier in 20 minutes); Sogepost, a mutual funds management company; Ardial, a security company guarding both cash and property; and Someposte and Sofreposte, technology companies specializing in postal logistics, project engineering and technology consulting and solutions implementation.

Finally, La Poste has developed subsidiaries that provide business mail services which complement conventional postal services and encourage customer loyalty: Dynapost, which offers businesses a total or partial in-house mail handling service, and Datapost, which offers a business mail service using computer data transmission linked to La Poste's postal network.

In Chile, internal transformation has taken the form of a flattened organizational structure that reflects a new management team's commitment to better strategic planning, streamlined internal processes and initiatives to incorporate up-to-the-minute technology linking 430 different offices throughout the country.

And in Italy, quality improvement measures are focused on a determination to raise levels of delivery previously far below European standards and levels of satisfaction that mirror the delivery results. By last spring, Ente Poste Italiane, the Italian post, had opened

15 urban postal centers on Sundays and had launched an ISO 9000 Total Quality project to raise the quality of the entire organization within International Post Corporation guidelines.

While all these initiatives reflect the imperative to become more business like in the face of increasing competition, none is a guarantee of success.

"It is not enough for governments and regulators to simply put in place commercial structures for their postal services," observed Thomas Leavey, the Director General of the Universal Postal Union, "and then hope it will follow naturally that their postal operators will operate in a more business-like way. We need to keep in mind that just as in any business venture, commercial freedom carries with it the freedom to fail as well as to succeed. The successful postal operator of tomorrow will therefore be the one that has listened to its customers and learned how to serve them better."

It's a lesson the United States is striving hard to teach itself.

### Listening to Customers — How the United States Transformed Performance

With the USPS organizational changes in place in 1994, three issues needed immediate attention: Chicago, where a new facility had to go on line without further disruption of service; Washington, considered the "conscience" of the Postal Service because of the proximity of so many important customers and members of Congress; and the onset of the 1994 fall mailing season. "We knew we were ill-prepared for the fall," said Henderson, "and we knew we had to allocate resources for all three areas." Allen Kane, who'd been appointed Vice-President in charge of Operations Support for the

Postal Service in February and who in the fall of 1996, was named USPS's Chief Marketing Officer, was asked to develop an operations plan for the fall season. Resources were dispatched to Chicago's and Washington's processing and distribution centers. It was there, Henderson's management team concluded, the answers to the questions confounding the mail delivery were most likely to be found.

Field senior managers had authorization to bring in whatever national resources were necessary, and before they were finished their reach extended to management, transportation and logistics experts. Critical additional distribution capacity and an operations support center were created. The results were dramatic, and continuously improving: for each of the next four quarters, external first-class mail "scores" (that is, how many local test letters got to their destinations in one day) set a record. "We wound up experiencing one of our most successful fall seasons ever," noted Allen Kane. "And the operations support center allowed us to both monitor daily performance, for the first time, and offer customer support to our big bulk mail clients. But what was most important was bringing the field into the process to both develop and implement our day-to-day strategy. Together, we shaped a two-pronged strategy: one, a focus on key service indicators; and, two, added infrastructure from skills and abilities, to transportation and dispatch discipline."

The Postal Service's next milestone would be to concentrate on the Washington Metro service, and Henderson again turned to Kane, and a dedicated team. By then, the field team had developed substantial research on the root causes behind 1993-1994's poor delivery record.

## Field Intervention in Washington

"I was a bit surprised to be called in," recalled Operational Specialist Kenneth Chapman, a 21-year Postal Service veteran who'd begun his career as a clerk at the Kennedy International Airport outside New York City, developed expertise in logistics, and had been moved to headquarters in Washington just that year. Chapman was teamed with Gary Thuro, a field intervention manager, and asked to head a Field Intervention Team (FIT) which would concentrate on the Washington Metro area. Although the Postal Service routinely tested delivery in 96 urban areas across the country, the District of Columbia was getting most of the bad press, and its quality of delivery had become a powerfully negative symbol. "But I had no preconceptions," added Chapman. "Both Gary and I brought a clear, fresh look."

Postal Service executives wanted the FIT to spend its initial efforts on fact-finding. The *Washington Post* had suggested that a dispirited, overcompensated, unmotivated workforce in the Metro area was deliberately delivering poor performance. As Chapman and Thuro moved from plant to plant, however, they began to conclude the problem lay elsewhere. Even at the Brentwood Processing and Distribution Center in northwest Washington, stigmatized in the press as the worst of the worst, the FIT met what they concluded were dedicated but frustrated professionals who desperately wanted improved performance.

For two weeks Chapman's and Thuro's team systematically toured the region's seven plants. "We were seeking feedback from the craft workers — the mailhandlers, the clerks, the machine operators and the truck drivers — which we'd compare with what we were seeing and hearing ourselves," remembered Chapman. Initial skepticism — the craft workers had seen plenty of management teams, and had rarely been impressed with the follow-up — gave way to the conviction that their voices were being heard. And the loudest message, decided the FIT, was that the performance measurements used in each plant didn't tell management much about actual day-to-day problems. The mail condition report was one example. Filed daily at seven am, the close of a Postal Service workday, the document would tell management the condition of the plant, and the pieces of mail that failed. But the report, noted the craft workers, never indicated when — or how — the evening's problems occurred. "If the cancellation is late," agreed one FIT member, "it affects everything else, from the machines, to the loading platform, to the trucks."

By the time the FIT finished its plant tour, four keys to success emerged: to achieve each daily operating plan; to make dispatches on time; to measure and improve distribution; and to put all the mail in vehicles and operate on schedule. "Our ability to gather meaningful, timely data on some of these basic measures," said Gary Thuro, "was the key to being able to take specific improvement action based on that information."

A second team — made up of employees from each of the region's seven plants — began meeting at the Postal Service headquarters' Operations Center. Their task: draft an action plan. "It was 'CustomerPerfect!' (the Postal Service's ongoing quality initiative, which is based upon the criteria used for the government's annual Malcolm Baldrige quality awards) in action," recalled Thuro. "The craft people saw the need to get back to basics, and to focus on fulfilling their customers' requirements."

The new task force was also given training in problem resolution. "Whatever expertise we wanted, we got," said Chapman. "The craft people began to believe they could make a difference."

"Allen Kane — together with a whole range of field managers — saw the need for coordination, hand-offs, and skill building," said Bill Henderson. "And, above all, the importance of meaningful, actionable measurements."

## Keeping Score

Performance tracking, the FIT and its craft worker team concluded, was the foundation upon which to build any successful turnaround. A "Metro Scorecard", using daily collected data, was the first step. Next came an "Issue Log", which tracked bottlenecks and other operational deficiencies. Any issue affecting performance would be added to the log. With the problem identified and solutions addressed, a manager could remove it from the document by initialing off. But if the issue remained, it went back onto the log, and another resolution had to be sought.

What the scorecard and log did was to empower the workforce to measure and report on itself. Executives assured their managers that honest reporting, rather than delivery problems, was what they intended to base evaluations on. "Trying to game the system," recalled Thuro, "would not improve performance in the long run."

The scorecard currently offers data at the performance cluster, district, plant and air mail facility levels. Within the plants themselves, performance is now measured on four criteria: operations to plan, or how well the night's assignment of equipment and personnel meets the demands of incoming and outgoing mail;

quality of distribution, an accuracy percentage reflecting a sampling of the night's sort; dispatch to plan, or how quickly the sorted mail was distributed and reached the loading platform for trucks; and vehicle load, which tracks the number and timeliness of the fleet's trips.

## The Turnaround

What the new measures began to reveal were broader issues, ones the individual plants — try as they may — needed to take an integrated approach towards. A regional transportation plan was necessary, as was a commitment to make certain that the entire network's equipment — the machines that made the sorts run on time — was operating to capacity. Kane allocated more resources: technicians to repair plant automation, and upgrade the employees' training on it; database improvement for better address management; transportation advisers to help with dispatching and routing.

After a few months, the root cause of the *Washington Post's* and Congress' complaints emerged: plants were holding back partially-full mail trays, ignoring the plan, so they wouldn't run short of vehicles. "Every truck that left a plant," said Chapman, "should have been taking as much processed mail as it could hold. But if a truck left empty, because it was scheduled to depart at 11 pm, we didn't know it." The scorecard simply indicated the truck had met its dispatch target. The mail handlers, said Chapman, forced themselves to change perspective. "They began to think of the trays holding letters as representing their customers," said Chapman. One tray, 500 customers. A thousand tray-capacity truck, carrying 100 trays, was a positive as long as the trays met the schedule. A truck with 900 trays, leaving late, wasn't.

This new approach needed a more sophisticated method of dispatching and routing, the craft worker team concluded. Henderson and Kane authorized $100,000 in start-up funding, and the team bought several message boards to hang in the plants. Programmed by computer, the boards would make a network distribution system visible, letting workers on the plant floor see when a truck had arrived, where it came from and where it was going, and what time it had to leave. Ten minutes prior to departure, the truck's listing would begin to flash, creating a sense of urgency. By last fall, the boards were up and running in several Washington plants. Now everybody held their breath, and waited to see if the performance numbers would follow suit.

**The Big Difference**

The good news was already circulating when in January, Jack Potter, fresh from the Massachusetts Institute of Technology's Sloan School, assumed control as the Metro area's new manager of operations. Morale, Chapman's FIT members could tell him, was up. Routine surveys showed line managers' stress, which had been measured at a nerve-wracking level, had dropped considerably. More importantly, the overnight delivery tests for local letters indicated dramatic improvement. Just before Christmas, in southern Maryland, 87 out of 100 local overnight letters were getting to their addressees in a day, a jump of 13 percent. Washington showed a similar increase, while Northern Virginia was up 11 percent. "There were skeptics who said it couldn't be done," said Postmaster General Runyon in the *Washington Post*. "But we did it."

Ken Chapman had already begun fielding calls from other areas of the country, asking for the secrets to the success. His outgoing mail was often filled with envelopes containing information about the scorecard and the issue log to not rely solely on the measurements. "One key to our success," he'd say, "was energizing the workforce to develop and maintain the critical information, and to deliver quality service to their customers." Focus on the customer, actionable information, and employee ownership of solutions were the other keys.

Potter, reaping the fruits of the renewed commitments and efforts of local management, had to agree. "The difference between this and other initiatives," says Potter, "is that our own people brought in the program, and that it is geared to what our managers wanted. There was no outside magic wand. There was, instead, a unified focus on the part of all our people in the entire Metro area to make this program work."

Loren Smith, then the Chief Marketing Officer for the USPS, said that growing awareness of the customer is an important breakthrough for any post. "Who the devil really is the customer?" Smith asked rhetorically. "Over the years I was in a position to call myself one of the largest customers of the U.S. Postal Service. But I never thought of myself as such a customer. As a matter of fact, I never thought about the U.S. Postal Service. Occasionally someone would come to me when I was involved with mailing and tell me a certain timetable or a certain schedule. But I didn't know anybody at the Postal Service was treating me as a customer. They were just a conduit to get something done that I needed to get done."

The internal transformation of the United States Postal Service had won another small victory in the battle for change. And the progress continued. In the fall of 1996, at another meeting with the USPS's Board of Governors, Marvin Runyon reported that the Postal Service was coming off its best two years in USPS history. Service quality had improved in seven out of the previous eight quarters, with performance scores at the time reaching into the low 90s. The previous two fiscal years had recorded the two largest net incomes ever, totalling more than $3 billion. Impressively, those nets followed the smallest rate increase in United States postal history, and the USPS was expected to keep those rates in place until 1998, at the earliest.

## Customer Perspective

"I was in a computer store recently," American Express vice president Laurel Kamen recalled, "and I realized that you can now buy equipment that will allow you not only to communicate across the world on the Internet, but that will also enable you to talk on the telephone through software on that same system. And once you communicate, you can transact. This intersects with postal issues in the most dramatic fashion."

We asked Kamen to reflect on the challenges faced by the postal industry – in particular those that emerge as a post struggles to commercialize in the face of growing competition. Keenly aware of the ongoing changes in the postal environment, Kamen noted that American Express has a presence online with ExpressNet, where cardholders can purchase travel and other services over their personal computers.

American Express, she said, had already consolidated postal sites, and operational and remittance centers. In several countries, mail processing centers cover multiple nations. The good news for the posts, said Kamen, is their internal recognition of the changing environment. Nowhere, she said, is it more evident than in the United States.

"In the past," observed Kamen, "the U.S. Postal Service knew that mailers had nowhere else to go.

Today, they see us going somewhere else and they're willing to work with customers to retain them." Indeed, a first-time partnership between American Express and the USPS resulted in the development of the FirstClass Phonecard, aimed at international visitors, and sold at most major post offices nationwide. The collaborative effort took just 88 days from conception to market. "We all went outside the box," said Kamen. "That's a new flexibility I've never seen before."

## In Conclusion: Mexico's Success

To compete, the world's posts have to think quickly, act quickly, and diversify. They're going to have to take on strategic alliances and partnerships. In Mexico, an alliance with Mailboxes, Etc. has allowed the capital-poor Servicio Postale Mexicano to open new suburban post offices for a key market that otherwise might be unserved.

As Mexico's Director General Gonzalo Alarcon recalled for us, "For or five years ago Mailboxes, Etc. visited us. We agreed to sign a contract with them so they would act as agents of SEPOMEX. We were very interested in the proposal because it was a way for SEPOMEX to have additional revenues, presence and coverage in places where we would not have been able to be located because of budgetary constraints. I am referring to the most exclusive residential and commercial areas of the main cities."

"Mailboxes, Etc. was able to do this," said Alarcon, "and deliver the services that SEPOMEX offers. So this looked very attractive and was one of the reasons we signed an agreement with them which we recently renewed for an additional six years."

Under the agreement, Mailboxes, Etc. sells stamps, mail boxes, parcels, and express mail services. Did the

Mexican Post, we wondered, get its fair share of the business of the outgoing parcels and expedited letters from Mailboxes, Etc., or was that business given to United Parcel Services, FedEx and DHL?

"If we had not joined with Mailboxes, Etc. someone else would have," said Alarcon. "We get a percentage for every franchise they sell and also from every product they sell. On the outbound we pay them a commission for selling our products (stamps, parcels etc.) and on the inbound, which is mainly parcels, is done through MexPostal Mexico and we make a revenue there."

The alliance with Mailboxes, Etc. has hardly been SEPOMEX's sole success. In recent years, delivery times have sped up, security improved, and service coverage extended to 97 percent of the country. MexPost and another new service, the Buzon Expresso, have strengthened the image and reputation of the Mexican post.

MexPost was inaugurated in 1989 as an express mail service delivering both parcels and letters. With agreements with TNT, Mailboxes, Etc. and others, MexPost accesses an international network and is already among the four largest courier and parcel services in the country. MexPost covers more than 750,000 international delivery points, serves more than 865 national points, and handled 2.6 million pieces in 1996's first quarter. By the close of 1996, MexPost anticipates having 160 trace system-equipped vans in operation.

Internationally, SEPOMEX has signed agreements with 76 countries, including a "global package service" agreement with the USPS. Other agreements include those with the Spanish post, the Portugal Postal Union and the Universal Postal Union. Internally, the Buzon Expresso — begun in 1992 — links all the major cities in the country through a 2,055-mail box network. That is expected to grow to 4000 mailboxes by 1997.

This increased capability is reflected in the numbers. In 1989, SEPOMEX handled 720 million pieces. Today, the post delivers 1,050 million pieces annually — an average five percent growth yearly. Meanwhile, SEPOMEX has put in place a systemwide employee training program, and posts an annual net profit, without government subsidy.

In Mexico, as in the United States and other countries whose regulatory environment had yet to catch up, the internal transformation is clearly underway. And it's already generating remarkable results.

# Chapter

# 4

## NEW ZEALAND AND CANADA—
## TWO STUDIES IN COMMERCIALIZATION

*By concentrating on our core business, by focusing on our business like any other corporation, we believe that we can play the game on a level field with our private sector competitors. That means meeting the needs of our customers, evolving with technology, paying taxes and dividends and achieving the commercial freedom to measure up to our goals.*
— Georges Clermont, President and CEO, Canada Post Corporation

Many lessons can be learned from the menu of initiatives by major national postal administrations in such countries as Argentina, Australia, China, France, Germany, the Netherlands, Sweden, the United Kingdom, the United States and Japan. They are all breaking new ground to increase their commercial freedoms, work with employees and unions, target their investments, become or remain profitable, separate commercial activities from their community service obligations, protect their exclusive privilege in law or in practice, partner with others, and redefine the way of managing the business to remain competitive.

New Zealand and Canada offer excellent case studies of posts which have commercialized successfully and — through their transformation — are well-positioned for the future, as long as governments don't interfere. In Canada's case, there's reason for concern, following the release in the summer of 1996 of a critical report of the Canada Post Mandate Review.

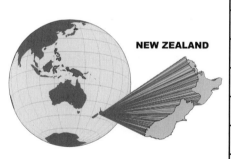

| | New Zealand (1995) |
|---|---|
| 1995 GDP (US $ Billions) | 61 |
| 1994 Population (millions) | 3.5 |
| Owner | Government |
| 1995 stamp cost (US$) | 27 cents |
| Employees | 9,284 |
| Revenue (US $ billions) | 0.42 |

## New Zealand Post Limited — Classic Transformation

In 1987, newly appointed New Zealand Post Limited (NZ Post) Chief Executive Officer Harvey

Parker dryly remarked that NZ Post was "Going places, down the gurgler." Less than ten years later, the NZ Post story is one of the most successful examples of the transformation of a former government department into a commercial enterprise.

In 1986, the New Zealand postal service, operating as a division of a government department, was losing nearly $40 million a year and forecasts were that this deficit would balloon to $50 million within several years. Today, NZ Post operates profitably in the form of a company structure and pays taxes and dividends to its shareholder the New Zealand government.

Customers have benefited with the price of the standard letter remaining unchanged for some years before being reduced from 45 to 40 cents in October 1995 — a step that has sent shockwaves throughout the industry — along with dramatic service level improvements (see Figure 4-1). In fact, the post has become so efficient and oriented to the customer that New Zealanders can send letters for free once a year, under the recently announced "FreePost Day" program, which allows any-

Figure 4-1

## NZ Post Standard Letter Postage
## (Before and After State-Owned Enterprise Act)

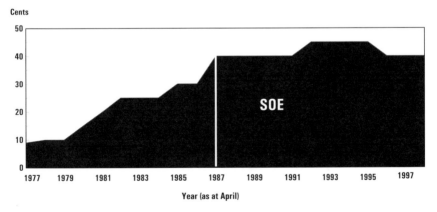

Figure 4-2

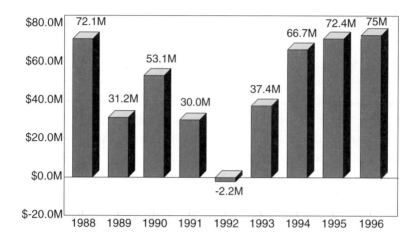

## NZ Post Profit After Tax

one to mail a letter at no cost as long as it is addressed by hand. Where once NZ Post reported consistent losses, it achieved a profit of $72 million after taxes in 1995 and $75 million in 1996, a return of average shareholders' funds of 35 percent (see Figure 4-2).

In the mid-1980s, NZ Post was facing a bleak future. The operation was very labor intensive with around 12,000 staff and 700 contractors employed. The asset structure was inappropriate: there were no modern mail processing plants, but there were 894 official post offices and 340 fixed-cost Agency post offices. Essentially, NZ Post's asset base was more appropriate for a retail banking operation than a modern postal business. Compounding its other systemic problems, NZ Post was being cross-subsidized by telecommunications profits. When this subsidy was removed, a 30 percent increase in core prices would be required if a break-even position was to be achieved. NZ Post was also suffering from a lack of strategic capital investment with little money spent on upgrading facilities and equipment.

How then did NZ Post reinvent itself so successfully that in November 1994 it was named "Company of the Year" in New Zealand?

This dramatic turnaround was achieved through a bold plan of commercialization undertaken by the New Zealand government. Because of the extent of the public debt problem and the level of inefficiency of the government's business activities by the mid-1980s, the New Zealand government implemented a new strategy to improve the performance of state enterprises and trading activities. The main thrust of the strategy was to achieve the potential efficiency gains of the full privatization without any change of ownership from public to private sector.

The most prominent feature of the strategy was the creation of nine government-owned corporations to manage and operate trading activities previously undertaken by government departments. The new corporations were responsible for such major activities as electricity, telecommunications, coal and postal service.

The legal framework for these corporations was articulated in the "State-Owned Enterprises Act" (SOE), which specifically required state-owned enterprises to operate as successful businesses and to meet three criteria — to be as profitable and efficient as comparable businesses that are not owned by the Crown; to be a good employer; and to be an organization that exhibits a sense of social responsibility by having regard for the interests of the community in which it operates and by endeavoring to accommodate or encourage these when it is able to do so.

Figure 4-3

> **NZ Post**
> **Business Principles**
>
> ❖ Sustained profitability
> ❖ Care for New Zealand by meeting defined social obligations
> ❖ Investment which adds shareholder value
> ❖ Valuing our people
> ❖ Reliable, efficient services at lowest cost and price

This new statutory framework was introduced for all state-owned enterprises to facilitate their improved economic performance and to enhance their accountability. The aim was to enable and encourage the boards of the enterprises to manage their businesses on a commercial basis, free from political control over day-to-day operations, while retaining ministerial powers to control the broad direction of corporate policies

At the core of the framework was the requirement for each corporation to prepare a statement of intent every year to cover six areas: the objectives of the enterprise and its subsidiaries (see Figure 4-3); the nature and scope of the activities to be undertaken; the financial performance targets and other measures by which performance can be judged, including pricing policy for corporations with monopoly power; the non-commercial activities for which compensation is sought from the government; the various financial measures and details of dividends to be paid to government; and other matters agreed between the shareholding ministers and the board.

Under the terms of this commercialization program, government has the opportunity to comment on and influence a draft statement of corporate intent, but, once everyone is agreed on the statement, the board of the enterprise is expected to be free to manage the business in accordance with the statement. The board is then accountable for its actions and performance as judged against the intentions set out in the statement.

The new framework has facilitated the introduction of private sector forces and disciplines into the management and operation of NZ Post. Top managers have been brought in from the private sector. Board members have been given commercial performance objectives and are expected to run the enterprise as a successful business. In the longer term, the post — like all corporations — is expected to eliminate all borrowing from government and borrow from the private capital markets in its own right. And the post is permitted to issue non-voting equity bonds, which enable non-government institutions and individuals to participate in the corporation while leaving ownership control with the government.

Given this new structure, recognizing the need for change and leveraging the government and public commitment to reform, NZ Post moved very quickly. Under Harvey Parker's stewardship, the new emphasis was on teamwork and managed commitment. His first move was to develop a management information and reporting system that was put in place in April 1987, two months after his appointment as CEO. A financial plan was quickly produced and the organization structure revised. A series of management committees was established which included a Senior Management Committee, Resources Committee, Personnel Committee, Corporate Communications Committee, New Products/Pricing Committee and a Staff Consultation Committee.

Next up was the task of putting in place an effective personnel system to effect the change process. NZ

Post's Human Resource Unit managed a process of restructuring that had numerous elements: downsizing staff count; emphasizing accountability and the drive for profit by managers; recruiting that focused on the best match of skills rather than seniority; and introducing a performance review system for management.

Figure 4-4

## NZ Post's Full Time Equivalent Labor Reduction

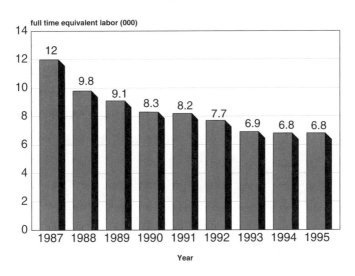

Following those steps, NZ Post achieved further gains in service standards by putting in place measurements to identify problem areas and resolve complaints. It also embarked on extensive automation projects (see Figure 4-4). By 1990, $120 million had been spent on a modernization and capital investment program. A critical element in this initiative was the establishment of efficient mail handling centers.

NZ Post has been a commercially aggressive business. In its quest for efficiency and reform, it has been required to make a number of difficult and unpopular decisions. This led to some concerns from Parliament that perhaps NZ Post reached decisions that compromised the role government saw necessary for a universal service provider. The government asked NZ Post to commit itself to defined social obligations in exchange for continued statutory protection.

This gave rise to the "Deed of Understanding", a contract between the government, represented by the Minister for Communications, and NZ Post (see Figure 4-5). The basic provisions of the Deed cover universal service, an indexed price cap for the standard letter, frequency of mail delivery, and size of the post office network.

Figure 4-5

**NZ Post**
**Defined Social Obligations**

❖ Universal price-equalized service
❖ Price control on standard letter
❖ Six-day delivery
❖ Minimum number of retail outlets
❖ No rural delivery fee

With the restructuring behind it, NZ Post developed strategies for long-term success. The post would protect its core mail business by continuing to look for ways to lower cost, and by expanding in the direct marketing and bulk mail and mail processing business.

A second strategic component would be to build — both within New Zealand and overseas — on NZ Post's foundation of skills, knowledge and experience through expansion in consulting services and joint ventures with other postal organizations.

Finally, NZ Post would protect the portion of market being eroded by electronics and support the efficiency of its core businesses, including retail financial transactions, through further development in electronic communications services. The post would transfer property management and development to a subsidiary company.

With his eye clearly focused on the future of NZ Post, current Chief Executive Officer Elmar Toime noted, "Now innovation in a company can mean many things. We can be innovative when we re-design business processes so as to improve efficiency or quality. We can be innovative in the way we train and develop our people, and how we then reward their creativity. And, of course, we can be innovative in how we provide products and services to our customers."

With that vision in mind, NZ Post has charted its course for the future, particularly in facing the challenges of new technology. "To protect against changes in letter mail usage, we broadened the range of services we have to offer," said Elmar Toime at a 1996 Coopers & Lybrand postal forum in Cannes, France. "Our ventures in telecommunications, electronic mail, and warehousing were among the first developed in the postal world." Volume electronic mail services have been developed with Datamail, a fully owned subsidiary of NZ Post. Datamail provided data-based computer services and intelligent mail processing including intelligent billing, imaging response processing and debt follow-up systems, processing over 10 percent of all letter volumes in New Zealand.

"For over a year, we have been living a different strategy we call *Farming the Core*," Toime revealed in Cannes. "This is a back-to-basics strategy. It says that in our core traditional business of letters, distribution, and counter transactions we can find the source of future growth and profitability for some years to come. The immediate consequence of this new strategy has been the divestment of two subsidiary businesses that we felt did not relate to our core." Lacking synergies that provided competitive advantage, Toime and New Zealand

Post's leadership team chose to simplify their business by reducing its activities. "Our business will not rely on an innovation strategy that diverges from what we define as our core," said Toime. "In my opinion, being able to quit a business also counts as innovation."

Other technology investments have included counter automation to provide value-added opportunities in payment receipting and agency services, the use of track-and-trace systems in its express courier service, facilities management, direct marketing and $12 million for development of a system to electronically read and sort addresses on machine-addressed envelopes.

In retrospect, NZ Post's dramatic transformation over the past decade can be explained by three key factors: the environment created; the structure selected; and the leadership provided.

First, the environment was designed to foster success. NZ Post was not only mandated to be commercial, it was given the tools and freedom to be commercial. The government granted NZ Post considerable freedom in such matters as pricing (other than the standard letter rate), marketing and personnel policies.

Second, a solid commercial structure was established. While the company was denied government guarantees to its borrowings and trading activities, a sound commercial structure was established following a year-long assessment and valuation of properties and assets.

Third, a structure for providing leadership was established. The government appointed a commercial board of directors, consisting of leading accountants, lawyers, and entrepreneurs. Political affiliation was not a criterion for selection. New managers were recruited, and existing ones received additional training.

These three factors have proven a winning combination as NZ Post has navigated a course to successful commercialization and stands poised for the challenges of the future. "At the end of June 1996," noted Toime in Cannes, "we announced a record profit for the second year in a row. This is remarkable because it followed some major price reductions earlier in the financial year." The Free Post Day, added Toime, had stimulated thousands of pieces of discretionary new mail. The SOE model, he said, put commercial decision-making in the hands of NZ Post's board and management, successfully separating commercial and shareholder issues from regulatory ones. Outside directors, and managers recruited from other businesses, provided an influx of new ideas, Toime pointed out.

"New Zealand," the post's chief executive concluded, "is in good shape, as is the postal sector in New Zealand. We know there is a strong future for the letter. We are the archetypical government-owned business. We do have defined social obligations, but we care about our public relations as a matter of prudent business. We support open markets and competition and we believe in market forces. We are certainly focused on commercial success."

| | Canada (1995) |
|---|---|
| 1995 GDP (US $ Billions) | 565 |
| 1994 Population (millions) | 29 |
| Owner | Government |
| 1995 stamp cost (US$) | 32 cents |
| Employees | 63,478 |
| Revenue (US $ billions) | 3.6 |

CANADA

## Canada Post Corporation — Customer Focus, Enterprise Success

Prior to 1982, the Post Office in Canada was a government department plagued by many of the systemic problems faced by other postal services. The Canada Post Corporation Act, passed in October 1981, was designed to transform the post office department into a business-like and self-sustaining Crown Corporation. By this legislation, Canada Post was mandated to deal with the serious concerns that had arisen over the service, labor relations, management and financial performance of its predecessor. "We concentrated on operational improvements," recalled Canada Post President Georges Clermont, "because we had to give people a reason to believe in the system. It was important, first and foremost, to show Canadians that their postal system could do the job and give them good service."

Since 1981, Canada Post Corporation (CPC) has dramatically reoriented itself to better serve its customers. It now sets, publicizes, and meets service standards, including delivery time commitments. In 1987, CPC became the first post to implement and publish the

results of an external, independent test of domestic let-
termail delivery performance. In addition, it has initiated a program of consistent monitoring of service
performance, enhanced customer access through franchising programs and has replaced the former "class"
system of service with a comprehensive range of dis-
tinct services that better meets the needs of customers.
All of these initiatives have helped to improve significantly the level of satisfaction among customers. "When
you've been a monopoly for well over 100 years," said
President Clermont, "it is difficult to instill a customer-
driven culture. We are dealing with attitudes and the
human mind. To build a successful corporation you need
satisfied employees to generate satisfied customers who
generate satisfactory financial returns. We have had to
work more on our employees and change the culture.
We launched a learning institute two years ago with
basic courses that everyone is going to."

At the same time, Canada Post's financial performance has improved steadily since 1981. During this
period, the basic letter rate has risen significantly less
than the Consumer Price Index — meaning that it has
fallen in real terms. As a result, Canadians now enjoy
letter prices that are among the lowest in the industrialized world. While holding down letter prices, CPC
recorded, in its 1988-89 fiscal year, the first profit of
Canada's postal service in more than 30 years. This
marked the end of the period of chronic deficits that, in
the final years of the Post Office Department, had
reached some $500 million annually. From 1989 to the
present, CPC has, in essence, been operating at a near
break-even level without any current need for taxpayer
support.

Since 1982, Canada Post's *processing* productivity
has improved 65 percent, primarily through the implementation of advanced processing technology. This has

been achieved despite the significant constraints of work rules in CPC's collective bargaining agreements. Work rules relating to collection and delivery also restrict Canada Post's ability to achieve productivity gains. However, in the same period, while points of *delivery* increased by nearly 30 percent, overall delivery productivity improved 24 percent largely through the introduction of community mail boxes and other similar equipment. "Postal administrations are not thought of as showplaces for modern technology;" said Clermont. "Our image is one of armies of people wearing green shades and black armbands, sorting letter one by one. The fact that a lot of very high-tech equipment was designed and manufactured to allow us to process 30,000 letters an hour does not enter the public's mind."

In 1994-95, Canada Post's annual net productivity gains reached approximately $573 million. This is equivalent to an average annual gain of one percent — double the rate achieved by the business sector of the Canadian economy since 1982.

However, CPC recognized that the long-term success of its commitment to affordable, universal service required a strong focus on cost containment and continuous service and productivity improvements. To ensure that focus, Canada Post established five corporate objectives for the future:

1) to enable the delivery of world-class services through the implementation of new human resource practices;
2) to be committed to service excellence by anticipating, responding to and exceeding customer expectations;
3) to earn sufficient returns to sustain and develop the business;
4) to build an environment that promotes full employee participation; and

5)  to be a leader in introducing innovative services that anticipate and respond to customer needs.

Canada Post recognized that the goal of delivering world-class service could only be achieved through the implementation of new human resource practices because CPC is a labor-intensive company: more than 90 percent of the employees are represented by four bargaining groups. While over the past decade significant progress has been made in improving the dialogue and relationship with employees and the unions that represent them, CPC concluded that more dramatic improvements are required.

Surveys of CPC employees have indicated that, while they have a highly favorable opinion of the corporation as a whole, there remain areas for improvement: more information about corporate plans and programs; opportunities to develop and realize employees' potential; and improved handling of workplace issues.

CPC recognized that, in the highly competitive environment in which it operates, retaining current customers and the revenue base associated with them would require improvement in customer satisfaction. Studies have confirmed the strongest link with customer satisfaction is employee satisfaction and that it takes twice as long to increase customer satisfaction as it did allow it to deteriorate. Benchmark studies have also confirmed the value of progressive and participative human resource management practices in delivering results to the bottom line. CPC took the position that improved financial performance correlates directly with human resources practices that go beyond participative management into the widespread application of incentive-based compensation.

After recognizing the relationship between improved employee relations and the future success of the corporation, CPC made a long-term commitment to provide employees with more timely information about the direction of the company, greater responsibilities for making business decisions, and the training and development necessary for them to be active in responding to the service and productivity objectives required to deliver world-class service.

The second objective — service excellence through anticipating, responding to and exceeding customer expectations — evolved from CPC's belief that its long-term survival depends in large part on its ability to change its business culture. CPC is seeking to develop a culture that is more customer-responsive: one that is able to react quickly to changes in the marketplace in order to take advantage of available business opportunities to provide customers with services that meet their changing needs. The corporation is reorienting its focus and restructuring how it interacts with customers to ensure excellence in all aspects of its service.

For example, despite statistical evidence that CPC's operating performance has improved significantly, other research shows that some customers — rural and northern Canada residents, small businesses consolidating their mail — still find CPC difficult to deal with. Large mailers, on the other hand, are relatively satisfied. In response, CPC is developing solutions to provide better billing and invoicing, improved mail tracking services and more knowledgeable retail staff.

Another important vehicle designed to assist in the process of delivering service excellence is the CPC Learning Institute, an education and training initiative that will support all employees in developing new skills and a better understanding of the challenges facing the company. The institute combines new programs with the best elements of existing training and development initiatives to place more emphasis on customer service, product knowledge and career development. In addition to delivering programs to employees, the Learning Institute sponsors research on new business trends, technologies and other areas that will help shape CPC's future. To contribute to the quality of the Learning Institutes programs, CPC works with Queen's University and Hautes Etudes Commerciales, two of Canada's most respected business schools.

Improving financial performance is the third objective. Over the past five years, CPC has operated, after adjusting for labor disruptions and real estate gains, at a break-even position and has depleted its cash position. In order to enhance its overall financial performance, CPC has used its cash, its proceeds from real estate dispositions, its borrowings and financing through operating leases to fund a significant program of investment to implement the required infrastructure necessary to revitalize its asset base.

To achieve its fourth objective, CPC is committed to building an environment that promotes full employee participation — and, by doing so, getting closer to the customer. CPC decided that decentralization was an important step in improving its relationship with customers and employees while, at the same time, realizing operational and administrative efficiencies. CPC is encouraging employee involvement through greater delegation and decision-making latitude. The goal is to equip and empower all employees to manage themselves and their areas of responsibility, to use a common-sense approach to resolving service issues and to respond to customer needs immediately, without having to comply with untimely or complicated processes.

As its fifth objective — and with an eye clearly focused on meeting customers' needs — CPC committed to becoming a leader in introducing innovative services that anticipate and respond to customer needs.

Throughout most of its history, the Canadian postal service has been in the business of transferring information between people, businesses and governments through a complex physical network of mail processing plants, retail outlets, people and transportation services. With the convergence of computers, electronic communication and interactive television, CPC has embarked on a program to deploy electronic network services that will complement and be integrated with its extensive physical network. Its ultimate goal: to offer universal access to both physical and electronic services.

As CPC prepares for the future, it does so knowing that it may face certain fundamental changes in how it operates. Canada Post stated its mission and needs to the recently appointed government commission to review its mandate as this: "We are in business to serve all Canadians, businesses and organizations through the secure delivery of messages, information and packages to any address in Canada or the world at a level of quality and value that makes customers want to repeat the experience. " To fulfill that mission, postal executives added, CPC had to realize eight needs — to be able to offer related products and services at market-based prices, to maintain a global reach and international access, to earn sufficient profits to sustain the business and pay dividends, to develop a culture that anticipates and exceeds customer expectations, to gain operating and contractual flexibility, to retain the letter monopoly and a timely mechanism for setting basic letter prices within inflation, to compete fairly, and to have both governance and a corporate structure appropriate to play those roles.

The Mandate Review, while solidly endorsing the need to provide a universal letter mail service at a uniform price protected by an exclusive privilege, did not agree with the provision of other competitive services.

The Review's commissioner expressed several concerns: that Canada Post's plans for achieving financial soundness were unconvincing; that it was competing with private sector companies from a position of strength the other businesses couldn't match; that the post was "overly aggressive"; that its strategic vision was to spread its activities ever wider through the private sector economy, losing its public sector focus; that its Minister, Board and the government had no way to provide necessary sustained supervision; and that its collective bargaining agreements were unrealistic.

Rather than explore or consider constructive ways of helping Canada Post move forward with its vision, the Review's commissioner drew on his expertise as a journalist to craft a case for moving Canada Post back into a narrow interpretation of its public service obligations. The Minister's public statements implied a government reluctance to move in this direction. The government will "study" the Review's recommendations and make its final decisions in the spring of 1997. Regardless of the outcome, it has been a frustrating process for Canada Post. It illustrates the problem of a public agency on a journey towards financial self-sufficiency and competitiveness. The competitors, not the customers, were starting to complain. The government now has to decide whether or not to continue the commercialization journey, or set back the clock, but it cannot freeze Canada Post in equilibrium.

CPC believes that its vision for the future best positions the post to provide the services Canadians will seek in the future and that the shareholder will, after reviewing all the options, support this vision. It is hard to disagree.

According to Hank Klassen, vice president of administration, the future looks promising for CPC. "What I see out there absolutely convinces me that we can compete effectively in an open market with the competition. It will take an aggressive management that's business focused and working on developing a culture that can very quickly change."

Adds George Clermont, "I would like to leave this company with a new culture, with an understanding of the customer, an understanding of the threats of competition, and the need to be competitive and what being competitive means."

# Chapter

# 5

## CORPORATIZING THE POST

"Our challenge for the future is, given such freedom and choice,
which markets should we be in?  Which products should we
eliminate?  We need to fit products to our customers
and balance our other roles."
—John Roberts, Chief Executive Officer,
The Post Office, United Kingdom.

John Roberts' lineage — postal, that is — traces back 480 years to the United Kingdom's first Master of the Posts, Sir Brian Tuke. Sir Brian's charge — to assure the safe carriage of King Henry VIII's mail in and out of London, and to make certain that mail reached the royal personage when the king travelled — is not dissimilar to Roberts' mandate to lead his government-owned corporation into the 21st century profitably and without subsidy. Both are (and were) complex tasks of great responsibility. Roberts, however, presumably does not face the dungeon (or worse) for missing his daily delivery targets.

The Post Office, born in its current structure on October 1, 1981, is perhaps the earliest modern example of corporatization in the postal industry. The Post Office had been established in the United Kingdom in 1969 as a nationalized industry after a ten-year modernization program that had included the introduction of national geographic codes, the installation of sorting machines to read the codes, and the tiering of letter service. Through the Seventies, The Post Office Corporation (whose market extended to telecommunications) refined and extended the coding of Britain, and in 1980, began to operate Intelpost, the world's first public facsimile service.

A government review of the postal business led to the 1981 decision to split apart telecommunications (which became British Telecom) and the post into two nationalized industries. Accompanying the restructuring were the beginnings of market liberalization: the letter monopoly could be relaxed, and work areas privatized, if The Post Office did not achieve and maintain agreed-upon levels of service quality, efficiency and profitability. "That year," recalled chief executive Roberts in the spring of 1996, "found our counters business in danger. A government review of the counters' business practices showed that based on its cost-plus pricing, one could construct a scenario where forty-to-fifty percent of the total business could disappear overnight." While there was risk in the restructuring, there was also the potential for reward. In 1986, The Post Office's Board of Directors announced a further restructuring to form five businesses, each with its own dedicated staff: letters, parcels, counters, Girobank (later sold to the private sector) and TV licensing, responsible for collection of the fees for television licensing. By 1994, the British government was considering a privatization — selling the letters and parcels businesses to the private sector, while retaining the counters — but dropped those plans later that year after intense public debate.

The Post Office's structure, then, remains much as it was in 1986. Royal Mail — King Henry VIII's personal post in 1516, but by 1635 accessible to the public (for the price of postage calculated by counting the number of sheets of paper and distance to be delivered) — collects, sorts and delivers mail and packets within the UK and overseas. Services include first- and second-class letter delivery at a uniform price to the country's remotest areas, as well as priority, insured and specialist business delivery services. Parcelforce, a leading carrier of packages, parcels and small freight, with a comprehensive range of domestic and international services for both business and private customers. And Post Office Counters is responsible for the operation of the nationwide network of 20,000 post offices, which is Europe's largest retail chain. Counters provides 160 different services, ranging from travel insurance and Kodak film collection to national lottery ticket sales and currency exchange.

The transformation of the counters business, said The Post Office's John Roberts, followed the 1994-95 debate on privatization. "The present commercial freedom of Counters would never have happened without that debate," Roberts observed. "They are transformed into a business that 'big brand' quality private companies want to deal with." With the interest of other companies has come opportunity to market a variety of products. However, all is not perfect. Constraints have been imposed by the government, and some commercial powers have been curtailed. That, said Roberts, is a challenge. "Given complete freedom and choice," Roberts stated, "which markets should we be in? Which products should be eliminated? We want to fit products to our customers and balance our roles as bank, benefits provider, travel agent, and retailer." New products, though, cannot be evaluated only on this basis. Besides customer and business needs, the Post Office must consider a third dimension: what will the government allow?

It's a dilemma that posts lacking the freedom of independent management and a liberalized market can empathize with. For the rest of this chapter, we'll focus on the story of Britain's Post Office — in our opinion, an outstanding example of successful transformation achieved within the freedoms and constraints of a corporatized entity.

## The Advantage of Corporatization

Many reasons may prompt a government to take steps toward corporatizing its public services. But first, let's redefine the term. Public-sector enterprises, such as posts — in response to changing demands made by the government, by customers, by the regulatory environment, and by competitors taking advantage of liberalizing initiatives within that environment — enter a process of transformation necessary for organizational survival. The first new phase is commercialization, which we addressed in Chapters Two and Three. The second is corporatization, a state in which the entity may be on a spectrum from one that remains under tight government control to one that is empowered to fund the organization from private facilities; in which management has near-autonomy to direct the organization in the dimensions of marketing, finance and operations; in which the market it operates within may become partially or substantially deregulated; and in which ownership of assets may be shared between government and the private sector.

Most often the desire to corporatize is borne of a need to become more efficient or the wish of the government to distance itself from the day-to-day running of the business. For some nations corporatization is a means to unbind public services from constraining political processes and legislation, enabling the organization to improve efficiency and cope with change more effectively. For a small but growing number of others, corporatization is a stepping stone towards complete privatization. While a corporatized organization is kept at arm's length from government but still "owned" by it, some nations—such as the Netherlands—have privatized many government services, including the post, and divested shares publicly.

Although government corporations that divest often realize vast improvements in efficiency, cost-control, self-sufficiency and competitiveness, the chances for failure are also increased dramatically. The safety net provided by governmental supports and subsidies is weakened if not completely removed.

Proponents of corporatization argue that the increased competition that usually goes with it spurs an organization continually to improve itself in order to perpetuate its existence. This is certainly a reasonable argument, but corporatization can be a double-edged sword. Public services — whether they be electricity, telephone service, health care or postal services — are designed to ensure that all citizens have access to these services and pay the same price for the service regardless of wealth or class. As a government's grip on public services loosens, former public organizations, now faced with open-market competition, may deem it necessary to eliminate basic services the masses depend on in the name of efficiency and cost-effectiveness. Achieving balance between universal availability of services and increased competitiveness and efficiency is crucial to any plans for corporatization.

The United Kingdom's postal service, the Post Office, has been corporatized for more than a generation, and the results have been outstanding. No longer a government department, the Post Office is a state-owned corporation with some of the autonomy of a private corporation. Post Office executives still argue—and we concur — that corporatization will only allow the business to go so far. The government's effective right of veto over commercial decisions, often for political reasons that have little to do with the business itself, continues to place a significant constraint on the market transformation of the organization. Greater commercial freedom in the business and the power to act without continual consultation would enable the business to more effectively achieve its vision of being a global communications company. The Post Office currently sits in a mid-point in the spectrum of corporatization we described earlier. They have no power to seek private funds and have not achieved autonomy in all market and operational matters. They have been allowed, however, to implement several significant commercial initiatives which would have been impossible to achieve as a government department.

Internally, the UK Post Office has achieved many transformational successes; the business is running well and setting a standard that many other countries could emulate. Impediments remain, including labor problems that have been exacerbated by a strike, but the business has made real progress that validates the decision to move from government department to corporate entity.

## The UK Post Office: A Model of Corporatization's Benefits

The decision to corporatize may be made as an effort to revitalize or revamp a financially troubled organization. The enactment of the British Telecommunications Bill in October 1981 split the Post Office Corporation, established in 1969, into two nationalized industries. The Post Office (posts and National Girobank) and British Telecom (telecommunications). Interestingly, the British post was not plagued with the internal cynicism or ridiculed by the external sarcasm of so many of its foreign counterparts. In fact, the Post Office was highly ranked in the public eye.

Nevertheless, in 1981 Prime Minister Margaret Thatcher launched an effort to streamline and improve public utilities, with the government initiating evaluations of all of the United Kingdom's public services. Today, the Post Office is organized as a commercial entity and is expected to make a return for its shareholder, the government. There are some significant differences, however, between it and a private organization or a corporation with full autonomy. The Post Office has an external financing limit which is similar to a dividend payment except it is set up to three years in advance and is cash- rather than profit-related. Post Office management is not allowed to borrow on capital markets and must rely on government approval for any significant investment initiatives. The Post Office must also set out its proposed strategy for the next five years in a corporate plan which requires government approval. Typically, the government has been reluctant to allow the Post Office to develop products significantly different from those it offers at the moment and has explicitly rejected the setting up of joint ventures or acquisitions.

In 1986 a new division of the Post Office called Post Office Counters was launched, and would eventually diversify the range of products and services available at the counters it ran. Now, Post Office Counters offer travel-related services such as currency exchange, insurance policies and limited banking services. Post Office Counters has tried to extend the product range further but has been constrained by a government unwilling to allow the business to take the commercial risk. The refusal to allow the business to develop a business line for potentially profitable product ranges such as airline and train bookings and theatre and concert ticket sales illustrates the lack of market autonomy the Post Office really has in its corporatized state. It can be contrasted with some of the freedoms given to divested organizations as illustrated in Chapter Seven.

Post Office officials — using the management freedom that corporatization has allowed — have introduced new technologies to address other equally provocative challenges. Royal Mail's management began preparing for the ever-increasing pace of communications that began in the late 1980s and exploded in the Nineties. E-mail, fax machines, computers and the Internet greatly increase the pace of communications. Merchants who once mailed catalogs to customers, waited for orders to be mailed back to the merchant, and finally mailed goods back to the customer can now place a catalog on the World Wide Web where customers can instantly e-mail their orders back to the merchant. The delivery of goods keeps pace with the speed of the shopping and ordering process.

The Post Office took an especially important step in the transformation process in 1986, when it was divided into separate business units (see Figure 5-1 for the current structure). Royal Mail comprised three-quarters of the new organization, with Parcelforce, Post Office Counters Ltd., and several smaller units making up the rest of the organization. In 1990, Parcelforce became a completely independent division, allowing it to focus on its unique function and to capitalize on its strengths, while being less encumbered by the regulations and procedures that bind a "do-it-all" organization. That same year, the United Kingdom government privatized its banking services (Girobank), and in 1992 the government said it might sell off Parcelforce. This was quickly followed by an announcement to carry out a structural review of the entire Post Office. The review findings were inconclusive and nothing really happened until the

## The United Kingdom's Post Office Structure [1996]

Figure 5-1

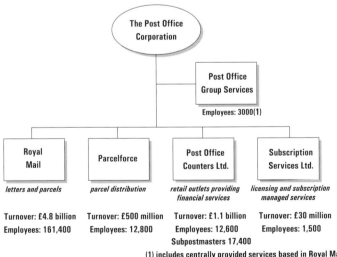

The Post Office Corporation

Post Office Group Services
Employees: 3000(1)

| Royal Mail | Parcelforce | Post Office Counters Ltd. | Subscription Services Ltd. |
|---|---|---|---|
| *letters and parcels* | *parcel distribution* | *retail outlets providing financial services* | *licensing and subscription managed services* |
| Turnover: £4.8 billion | Turnover: £500 million | Turnover: £1.1 billion | Turnover: £30 million |
| Employees: 161,400 | Employees: 12,800 | Employees: 12,600 | Employees: 1,500 |
| | | Subpostmasters 17,400 | |

(1) includes centrally provided services based in Royal Mail

Green Paper in 1994 proposing that Royal Mail and Parcelforce be sold together while keeping Post Office Counters under public control.

The privatization idea scared off too many members of Parliament to succeed. But, with the earlier division of the Post Office into specialized business units, its management continued a series of initiatives begun in 1988 toward total quality management. Paramount in this initiative was a renewed emphasis on customer service. In early 1989 Royal Mail launched a program called Customer First, in which a promotion of external customer focus enabled it to identify new products and services as well as develop means to measure customer satisfaction from both quantitative and qualitative standpoints.

Of course, customer satisfaction is an elemental ingredient to any successful business, but it is only part of the recipe. Crucial to a new emphasis on customer service is ensuring that both management and front line staff (employees who deal with the public on a daily basis) are satisfied with their jobs. In fact, employee satisfaction was a critical element of Royal Mail's plans for business development. "None of our managerial staff were staying in the same jobs," noted John Roberts. "It was essential that they understood the changes that were happening as we were not only expecting them to move jobs but in a number of cases move locations and homes."

Underlying Royal Mail's plans for development was the understanding that while changes — improvements in efficiency and effectiveness, changes in rules and regulations, and increasing emphasis on customer service — were attainable, the benefits of these changes would not be fully realized unless Royal Mail also made major shifts in the attitudes and values of the organization. Employees themselves had to embark on an ambitious change, and even today, John Roberts emphasizes that success depends on individual performance and attitudes.

"We have lots of people," he says. "But we employ individuals, not battalions. Our success or failure rests on how well we handle these individuals. How do you communicate and motivate? Parcelforce is emerging through a more market-focused, devolved structure, directing responsibility at local level towards meeting customer requirements, and gearing [itself] more closely to the needs of individual market sectors."

Royal Mail set a strict timeline on its organizational transformation to allow little time for the uneasiness and uncertainty that often comes with change. From inception of this restructuring in late 1990, less than two years were planned for the program to be in place and running throughout the United Kingdom. In this short time, Royal Mail set strict goals to measure its success. The key was an effort to emphasize the immediate benefits of restructuring to meet total quality.

Royal Mail's directors identified three crucial themes in the company's business development plan to ensure that the new Royal Mail would be accepted and embraced by its employees. Those three foundations were teamwork, involvement, and empowerment.

The directors also abolished the traditional, leveled hierarchies of old-style business in the new corporate structure. Royal Mail's priority shifted to a team-oriented strategy focused on employees who deal with customers on a daily, personal level. Management's role was no longer to decree policies from afar and enforce them among the lower ranks. Instead, middle and upper management's role was and is to listen to the needs of the front-line staff and react immediately to customer demands. Management and front-line staff remain united in their efforts to provide ever more efficient service.

Before, during, and after the installation of a business development plan Royal Mail needed to involve a cross-section of all levels of the organization in the decision-making process. Again, the goal was to implement change swiftly and effectively. Royal Mail's employees were made fully aware of the direction in which the business was heading. They all understood the tenets of total quality. Employee involvement in the early stages of the program also became an example for managers. They in turn involved their staff in a myriad of the business's activities, from corporate headquarters to the village post counter.

Boldly, Royal Mail eliminated constricting sets of rules and regulations in favor of a set of much more loosely defined guidelines. This freedom enabled managers to exercise their own judgment in coping with changing customer demands, logistical challenges, and employee relations. In a rapidly shifting business environment the removal of traditional chains of command is critical to an organization that is constantly evolving. With these increased powers at Royal Mail came increased accountability for decisions and actions.

Throughout the post-corporatization evolution of the Post Office, advances made possible by technology continued to drive the company's transformation. Of course, posts that have not corporatized benefit from these advances as well. But by taking adroit advantage of them, the Post Office has positioned itself well to meet the new challenges on the global postal horizon. Moreover, the fact of the Post Office being corporatized has enabled it to respond more swiftly to technological change, so there is a synergy to the situation not possible in more conventional posts.

## A View From Within: Parcelforce's Kevin Williams

Parcelforce's managing director, Kevin Williams, agreed to share his insights on the transformation of the UK letters and parcels businesses into major international players in the industry. Williams was in the privileged position of being a driver of the changes in Royal Mail after which he was appointed Managing Director of Parcelforce. He then employed the concepts that had worked well in Royal Mail and built on them to accelerate the existing change process in the parcels business. The initiatives in Royal Mail, he recalled, first began to emerge in 1988 following that year's postal strike. "We needed to improve the way we led our people and raise their level of job satisfaction whilst improving quality," Williams began.

"The main goals were to increase flexibility and teamwork, to develop an enterprise culture, and to put in place an integrated HR strategy that would support the delivery of business goals," Williams recalled. "The three key HR objectives were to develop a culture where change could be implemented speedily and effectively, develop capable and committed employees, and introduce working practices, and reward strategies which enables us to meet business goals. The barriers to change were, and still are the lack of shared goals and values with our employees and their representatives and no perception by managers and employees of a pressing need for change."

How does one surface the awareness of the need for change? we asked Williams.

"Generally, it is harder to convince employees of the need for change when profit and revenues are increasing. At that time, as now, Royal Mail was performing well financially," Williams answered. "In these circumstances people look for a pressure for change such as competition, imminent financial disaster or shareholder demand. Our employees saw none of these. But our research pointed to future threats coupled with the possible dilution of the monopoly protection afforded to 50 percent of Royal Mail's volume. So the pressure for change had to be generated internally against future threats. That's a tough challenge. You're asking people to take a leap of faith, to join you in a pre-emptive move to beat competition that is effectively growing but still out of sight."

Under these conditions, the letters monopoly becomes a double-edged sword, suggested Williams. Its protection of revenues actually makes overcoming the natural resistance to change in people far harder. "It may seem a strange point to make," conceded Parcelforce's managing director, "since most companies expend enormous effort to try to achieve a monopoly position. But they have a de facto monopoly which is always liable to threat whereas we have an apparently impregnable de jure monopoly, which can be an inhibitor of change. If we fail to convince our people of the ever-present need for major change, it could actually lead to our downfall.

"We introduced a variety of programs in Royal Mail," Williams continued, "to prepare our people for change at the same time as trying to emphasize that the status quo was not the way forward.

"The first program addressed the people and cultural issues," he said. "It focused on training in leadership skills and the restructuring of remuneration and working practices. To give employees a stake, our earnings strategies needed to reflect performance and how well the organization was meeting its objectives. We also spent considerable time working with the trades unions to improve relationships at all levels and the procedural framework governing these relationships."

Employee education followed. "Royal Mail has implemented a package called 'Understanding the Business'," said Williams. "This is designed to raise awareness of key business drivers and the need for change. It has been delivered to all employees in small groups which is a major exercise in an organization employing 150,000 people.

"The Post Office as a whole is one of the last trading portions of the public sector and is a huge employer with around 200,000 employees," observed Williams. However, at the end of the 1980s a culture of enterprise did not penetrate all levels within Royal Mail or any of its sister businesses. "Only at the Managing Director's desk did profit come into focus," he said. "Royal Mail was functionally-driven and operationally-focused, with costs and revenues driven by separate management organizations. The second program tried to correct this."

That program had six key objectives: to save overheads; create decentralized profit centers; raise the capability of the workforce; increase teamwork; develop a market-focused organization and reduce the size of the head office. Its achievements were considerable: the creation of 19 business units from 64 cost centers; the reduction of strategic headquarters staff from around 3,000 to 160 employees; the formation of Royal Mail Consulting, a central services organization; the shedding of 3,500 white-collar jobs at an annual saving of £65m; and the introduction of market-facing units serving a segmented customer base with sharply differing customer needs.

"In the old organization," remembered Williams, "customer-unfriendly actions were not unusual because our functionalism not only drove them but unwittingly rewarded them through incentive schemes. For example, a salesman winning one million pounds' worth of business received plaudits, but to his operations counterpart was a source of trouble as his expenditure budget was blown. One was focused on revenue gains, the other on a relatively fixed cost target."

The new structure created profit centers where sales and operations worked together and put in place processes to get teamworking into the business. And the change process covered the complete spectrum of issues — structure, processes, culture, innovation.

"A difficulty for any business," said Williams, "is when the pendulum swings between economies of scale and synergy and focus and devolution. We want to seize the middle ground but experience suggests that focus and economies of scale are uncomfortable bed fellows. Some would say not uncomfortable but impossible".

With real accountability and process-based working, said Williams, customer service soared. "The downside," he admitted, "was a bit of going native as divisions increased autonomy. The prize of commercial -ization was the loss of effective sharing. Some would not embrace a best practice if it wasn't 'invented here'."

At Royal Mail, Williams said, it's "hold your nerve time."

"We must persist with the culture of enterprise," he observed, "but be tougher on difference where it is not necessary. We need maturity and conformance to agreed standards coupled with a continuous improvement approach that drives up accepted norms which become the new standards."

Parcelforce's transformation, he said, has been a somewhat different story.

"I was in the privileged position of having done it before [in Royal Mail], with a year's hindsight to reflect on what could be improved before we started making changes here," said Williams. This transformation was born out of the commercial imperative to cut overhead, which was more prominent than at Royal Mail as Parcelforce was loss making, in addition to other important objectives - the creation of a profit culture, market sectors to replace product focus and an end to free issue. Success was dramatic. Savings of £13m, about 30 percent of that addressed, were secured. A clear market focus emerged through restructuring into eight geographic business units and eight market sectors. Non-line activities — finance and payroll, for example — were clustered into central support service centers. Segmented sales channels were formed to support the market sectors, creating concentrated sources of innovation in tailored product development and specialist selling.

After 18 months, Williams thinks he has a firmer sense of direction for transformation than he'd felt at Royal Mail. "I have learnt from these changes," Williams said. "I have brought in high quality outsiders to improve our people stock. By becoming closer to our customers, we've seen ways to solve the quality/cost/revenue balance dilemma."

**Technology as a Driver**

Technology continually creates real opportunity for Royal Mail, in part because the company can respond positively rather than defensively to new developments. Royal Mail is now marketing itself to businesses as another ingredient in their advertising and marketing formulas. By rapidly developing and introducing new products and services Royal Mail is keeping up with customer demands. Improvements in consumer services such as same or next day delivery are keeping customers faithful.

From home catalogue shopping to high volume trading and shipping of merchandise, technology will continue to speed the way in which businesses communicate. While much of the volume of information exchange can be handled electronically, Royal Mail has recognized that there will need to be paper copies of invoices, account statements, and order forms for many years to come. In order for postal services to survive they will need to keep in step with the swiftness of electronic data exchange. Royal Mail has done just that. While electronic information exchange is highly reliable there will always be glitches. When a problem occurs, users rely on hard copy to ensure accurate transactions. However, as businesses become more accustomed to the speed of computers and fax machines, the need for rapid delivery of paper will grow.

With the continued fragmentation of consumer demands into highly specialized markets, Royal Mail has also recognized that there is a substantial need for database development and management. In fact, Royal Mail is capitalizing on this immense opportunity.

In developed economies everywhere, the computer is rapidly transforming how people live and work. The small or home office is decentralizing the traditional corporate office workplace. This is generating new collection needs, delivery requirements, pricing schedules and posting needs. Royal Mail has structured many of its services and products to take advantage of these changes.

Today, as Royal Mail has realized, technology is also rapidly transforming the banking industry. The traditional bank with counters and tellers is quickly becoming an anachronism. First, automatic teller machines allowed customers to make simple transactions at any time of day. With the proliferation of computers in the home, bank customers with a direct deposit account through their employers can connect to their bank to check balances, pay bills, and transfer funds without leaving their homes. The chore of paying bills—writing out checks, stuffing them in envelopes, affixing stamps, placing them in a mail box, and balancing the checkbook— is replaced with the click of a button.

Though home banking is not yet used by many people, it may soon be a major threat to a large portion of the world's first-class postal market. How does the Post Office then compete with the electronic threats to its business? Royal Mail has asked itself this very question. Royal Mail's marketing director, Jim Cotton-Betteridge, perceives technological advances not as threats to the post's survival but—if the business is able to adapt—the means to continually improve what it does.

"I guess where I am coming from is this. It is easy to spot the areas, the markets which are going to go away or going to be changed in the electronic age," Cotton-Betteridge says. "It is perhaps not quite so easy to spot some of the opportunities. However history tells us that communication breeds communication and it is already clear that electronic media can generate more mail than it cannibalizes."

Royal Mail views the dramatic changes in global communications resulting from technology not as threats to its business but as a means to developing potential markets. Business is not lost as a result of electronic information exchange; rather, business is being generated. Every new cable TV subscription, cellular phone service contract, or Internet service account generates ten to 20 new pieces of mail annually.

The computer itself is responsible for increasing amounts of mail. Seventy-five percent of the mail written today is created on a computer, and over 90 percent of that is still delivered conventionally as mail.

Technological advancements are also changing the way Royal Mail handles postal items.

Royal Mail is developing sorting capabilities that will allow its equipment to sort down to an individual person's location within a business. Additionally, the company is developing capability for products that will allow mail forwarding to alternate locations on specified days — for example, when someone is on vacation or at a conference.

Royal Mail is also considering systems to convert mail to an electronic image. In these systems, mail can be opened, electronically photographed, transmitted to another post office, and printed or delivered electronically into an office mail system. Currently, Royal Mail is the only organization in the United Kingdom with the infrastructure to offer these services to private individuals.

## How Technology Can Drive Customer Service — The FastTrack Example

In 1993, Royal Mail — pressured by the conflicting needs of key customers wanting late access and others demanding early next-day delivery — began to look closely at the progress of a letter through one of its processing centers. When the results were announced, postal officials were shocked.

A stamped letter, on average, spent approximately two and a half hours working its way from entrance to final selection. A metered letter moved slightly faster, taking roughly 135 minutes. The surprise, the Royal Mail's tests showed, was the route a typical letter took. Mapping the processes affecting each piece of mail in a center, UK postal executives saw that a letter spent less than two minutes in value-adding activities — segregation, coding and sorting. The rest of the time, the mail was waiting after processing, sitting in heads of work (containers awaiting treatment), waiting in queues, or moving long distances between operations. None of that, officials realized, added any value.

"We needed to speed up throughput times at each processing stage in the network," recalled Alan Goddard, currently the Director for Letter Post at An Post in the Republic of Ireland. "That would give a better quality of service by getting more items to customers on first delivery." It would also lead to further examination of delivery options.

Goddard, at the time the Director for Processing at Royal Mail, became one of the first sponsors of an experiment called FastTrack, an effort to address a global need of postal authorities continuously seeking to meet more demanding network requirements.

Goddard and others knew advanced technology for segregating, coding and sorting mail in high volumes had helped, but that processing centers still often failed to meet their network deadlines, or that sub-optimal network arrangements were employed to meet the clearing capability of processing centers.

Royal Mail's solution to this dilemma was FastTrack: an innovative adaptation of performance improvement principles widely applied in the manufacturing industry. FastTrack — conceived in partnership with Coopers & Lybrand Consulting — focused on improving three operational areas: throughput (the passage of a letter through a process center) time; throughput rate; and process control.

## Streamlining the Throughput

In mail processing, postal authorities understand that time is essential. The longer a letter takes to work its way through a processing center, the longer the delay before operators can close down the final selection and prepare the mail for dispatch.

The FastTrack techniques challenged the reasons for this non-value-adding time and developed new ways of working to reduce it, reducing the overall throughput time for the letter. Senior management laid out the plant and equipment to introduce time-based control points.

The floor layout of many processing centers often had grouped culling, facing and cancelling machines (CFCs), optical character readers (OCRs), and letter-sorting machines (LSMs) in different parts of the building, even on different floors. FastTrack forced a rethink on the layout to form flow lines — for example, a CFC feeding an OCR feeding the LSMs for each mail stream. This arrangement reduced the non-value-adding handling and waiting time and travel distances within the center, and eliminated the need for staging large quantities of mail.

Even with a new layout, the need still arose to proactively manage the flow of mail to avoid delays. A manufacturing industry approach used volume-based control points (or KanBans) to do this. The postal industry, however, has considerably less influence on its raw material supply than its counterparts in manufacturing, yet must still clear the mail each evening. In these circumstances volume-based control points don't work.

To proactively manage the flow of mail between operations, FastTrack implementers needed to introduce time-based control points, in which an operator moves a pre-determined volume of mail every five minutes. When stoppages occurred in machine-controlled processes for whatever reason, this five-minute movement continued by diverting to or from another stream, ensuring continuous flow of mail through the center.

The results were impressive. Royal Mail's FastTrack trial programs established throughput times of 45 minutes. Those centers achieved a higher proportion of mail on relief dispatch and full clearance each evening, improving the quality of service and giving the opportunity to introduce a more optimal network.

The introduction wasn't easy, cautioned Alan Goddard. "Don't underestimate the difficulty of persuading old school managers to embrace this modern approach," Goddard said. "There is generally an inbuilt inertia amongst middle and junior management against embracing such radical changes in operating practice. Do it first in a unit that is keen to be involved and is manageable in size terms. Likewise don't first do it in one or two places, write the instruction manual and send it to other sites for them to follow. It won't work. The whole FastTrack methodology needs to be owned and embraced at each site. It has to be deployed in a controlled way with professional expertise. Every element has to be incorporated - cherry picking will seriously sub-optimize. Deployment needs to be controlled and disciplined to make it work. But when it does, the operational quality and financial benefits across the whole mail pipeline can be immense."

**Altering the Throughput Sequence**

The advanced technology at Royal Mail's processing centers used for segregating, coding and sorting mail had the capability of processing letters at very high rates, often in excess of 30,000 items per hour. However, measuring the actual rate of mail per clock hour through the total sequence of operations showed an overall throughput rate considerably less, often as little as 20,000 items per hour, even at peak times.

In any processing sequence of operations, one will determine the highest rate at which mail can flow (see Figure 5-2). Which operation could support which rate had to be determined to help improve its effectiveness to determine the highest possible throughput rate for each mail stream. With that information, the test centers could modify, as necessary, all other activities upstream and downstream from that operation to achieve that highest possible rate through the sequence.

These activities included the afternoon and evening collection activities which bring mail to the processing center for outward processing. Typically, UK (and other) postal authorities design their collection routes to optimize use of vehicles and/or staff time. They regarded the evening peak as normal and unchangeable, even though it clogged the processing center at a critical time.

FastTrack challenged those assumptions. Experience within Royal Mail had shown that focusing collection activities on the needs of the processing center to have a more even flow of mail could bring sub-

Figure 5-2

## Typical Arrival Pattern
## Before and After FastTrack

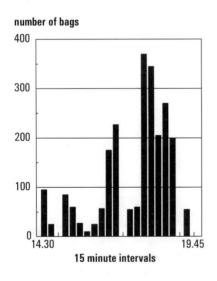

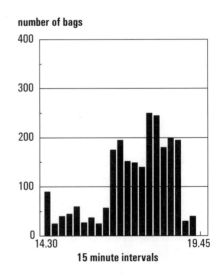

stantial volumes of mail into the center earlier at little additional cost.

By changing the arrival pattern and reducing the evening peak, FastTrack created capacity to handle additional mail volume and allowed later access for key customers.

In addition, because of the FastTrack focus on achieving the highest possible throughput rate for each mail stream, and matching the arrival pattern as closely as possible to it, it became  easier to identify and deal with any overloads early in the shift  to maintain the smooth processing of mail through the center.  As a result, the throughput rates after FastTrack implementation increased significantly while costs fell because of consequent changes to shift patterns and staff duties.

## Process Control

In many industries, the use of high value capital equipment isn't highly effective, where measured in both efficiency and utilization. The postal industry is no exception.

The advanced technology used routinely by most postal authorities has revolutionized the mechanical processing of mail.  But when letters drop out of this mechanical stream at any stage during outward processing, throughput time grows and throughput rate drops because of the need to sort manually. Mechanical sorting on inward or walk-sort is precluded, adding to costs and delays, and potentially reducing the quality of service.

FastTrack incorporated techniques designed to analyze these mechanical processes in detail and to identify the steps necessary to eliminate such drop-outs. After applying this analysis, the processes invariably performed to a higher level of efficiency, ensuring more mail coded and sorted mechanically, and supporting the achievement of the throughput time and throughput rate objectives at lower cost.

Any post can emulate Royal Mail's success by applying the range of FastTrack techniques. With FastTrack, postal authorities can provide a better quality of service in terms of both access and delivery by linking their islands of automation and mechanization, and by using them more effectively, by producing a more consistent flow of mail and achieving earlier ready-for-dispatch times, and by creating a more satisfying work environment at reduced cost.

"FastTrack provides a range of benefits which can be taken in a combination of different ways to suit local as well as national requirements," agreed Alan Goddard. "It gave Royal Mail opportunities to bring forward dispatch times to suit key network requirements, and provided a window at the end of the processing deadline to cope with unexpected surges. I also liked the in-process measures that FastTrack brings. These provided an absolute measure of volume at every point of the process every five minutes as a result of the time-based control points. This gave us tight floor control, but more importantly perhaps, devolved decision making on flow control to front line staff which freed up more supervisory and management time, allowing them to manage the overall process more effectively.

"As well as the customer service and quality benefits we got from FastTrack across the entire collection to delivery pipeline," concluded Goddard, "there were other spin-off benefits from FastTrack within the processing centers. These included space savings from avoiding the clutter created by containers of work awaiting treatment, and savings on rework and handling, which lead to direct financial benefits. In addition the robust implementation planning systems used as a key element of the FastTrack approach to control the implementation program produced great team commitment within the center, and helped drive the whole change process."

## Sustaining the Advantage

The great success of the Post Office's corporatization was evident almost immediately after the inception of its business plan. Royal Mail realized savings of nearly £65 million annually. Substantial cuts in staff saved even more money while causing only minimal disruption to the daily operations of the organization. As Parcelforce managing director Kevin Williams noted, Royal Mail's headquarters was reduced from a centralized support structure with a staff of 1,700 to a strategically oriented leadership team of just 162 staff. Several business development units arose from the need to focus closely on individual components of Royal Mail's highly divergent market. The perception of Royal Mail by business users shifted from that of a sluggish government service to a quality, name brand business like UPS or DHL.

Understanding what the customer thinks of the organization, confirmed Post Office chief executive John Roberts, is paramount. "We monitor people's perceptions of us very closely," said Roberts. "Royal Mail is continually scored as the highest-rated utility in the United Kingdom and Post Office Counters is not far behind. But we do need to get a lot sharper in our focus on the business. Our customers still see some of our business-pricing techniques as anachronistic and unsuited to the commercial world."

That, and other challenges remain. Pricing of some services and products remains under government regulation. Retail efficiency can still be elusive, and a measure of the partnering with the private sector would perhaps be more effective were Royal Mail privatized. Nevertheless, Royal Mail and the other lines of business of the Post Office have achieved substantive change.

Of course, the United Kingdom's Post Office is not alone in the strides it has made through corporatization. As we shall see next in our examination of the transformation of the posts in Denmark and Germany, corporatization is an international phenomenon. Furthermore, there are interesting developments in these and other countries that complement but do not replicate some of the Post Office's advances, notably in such partnering ventures as Deutsche Post's subcontracting of its long distance parcels transports.

As a result of its foresight in corporatizing, the Post Office in the United Kingdom is widely regard as a first-class company and a benchmark for post offices throughout the world. But it finds itself now at a crossroads as it faces ever greater competition from other posts and from courier companies and electronic communications. How it meets these challenges will define the future success of the Post Office as it enters the new millennium.

# Chapter

# 6

## GERMANY, DENMARK AND MALAYSIA — THREE STUDIES IN CORPORATIZATION

*I am absolutely convinced that we will be able to satisfy our
customers in the future by offering an attractive range of services.
However, we must continue to improve our services and add
innovative touches. As an organization that is still learning how
to operate in a market economy, we must continue to enhance
quality and customer benefits.*
— Dr. Klaus Zumwinkel, Chief Executive Officer,
Deutsche Post AG

As we have seen, the road to corporatization can take many different turns. And, as posts become more like businesses, they each face different sets of complex influences that an open marketplace puts on enterprises. Three posts that have successfully moved to the corporatization phase of structural transformation — Germany, Denmark and Malaysia — have followed different paths and timelines, and face different futures.

The governments of these three countries have spent much of the past decade or more studying the advantages of structural transformation. Given the unique circumstances surrounding the corporatization of their posts, it is revealing to examine how each has transformed itself into a corporatized enterprise and how it envisions its role in the coming years.

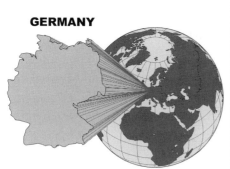

**GERMANY**

|  | Germany (1995) |
|---|---|
| 1995 GDP (US $ Billions) | 1,903 |
| 1994 Population (millions) | 81 |
| Owner | Government |
| 1995 stamp cost (US$) | 61 cents |
| Employees | 341,910 |
| Revenue (US $ billions) | 18.7 |

## The Deutsche Post Experience — Systematic Transformation

The German government has consistently pursued a reform timeline that began with "Postal Reform I" in 1988. This early initiative separated postal, banking and telecommunication services. On January 1, 1995, "Postal Reform II" commercialized the postal service as

Deutsche Post AG by making it a fully-owned government corporation. The government is currently preparing outlines for deregulation and share offering and privatization in the reform's final phase, "Postal Reform III," to be completed by the end of this decade.

In preparation for further reform, the postal minister recently unveiled an outline of legislation which would begin deregulating the postal market in 1998 and introduce full competition in 2003. Prior to the outline's publication, Deutsche Post's leadership indicated in March 1995 that the organization should be able to float shares on the German stock exchange in 1998.

As Wolf Dietrich Filter, Director of Letter Mail Processing, stated on behalf of Dr. Klaus Zumwinkel, the German post's chief executive officer, at a 1995 international postal forum, "Deutsche Post has taken on the challenges. Its transformation and innovations have successfully brought Deutsche Post AG along the path toward becoming a customer-oriented and competitive company. We have proceeded systematically and very much with the target in mind of developing and implementing a strategic transformation required of the company."

In the fall of 1996, however, in Cannes, France, Dr. Zumwinkel offered a cautionary comment. "We have prepared ourselves for competition within the framework of the strategic reorientation of our company," the Deutsche Post AG chief executive said. "We have made heavy investments in the future and implemented state-of-the-art production systems. We have considerably enhanced the quality of our services, yet have managed to reduce costs at the same time. This good starting position should not be jeopardized carelessly by unfair competition — that is, by liberalization without reducing the company's historical and infrastructural burden at the same time."

So successful has been the Deutsche Post AG transformation that in 1994, for the first time since German unification, the post recorded a positive result for its ordinary business activities which amounted to DM 257 million, a marked increase of DM 429.5 million over the previous year. The result for 1995 grew further, to DM 364.0 million. As Filter went on to say, "Admittedly, this has not been easy, but as the saying goes, 'No pains, no gains'.

## How Deutsche Post Transformed Itself

With the passage of Postal Reform I, Deutsche Post began to face the new challenges of a liberalized competitive environment. To keep itself on-track to corporatization, three corporate goals were established as main business objectives: 1) to offer quality that met top international standards; 2) to develop a private enterprise organization for customers and staff members; and 3) to become and remain a financially sound company, while fulfilling social obligations.

All subsequent measures were oriented to these main objectives. Divisional strategies covering all business segments — letter mail, freight mail, international mail and postal retail outlets — were developed and would be supplemented and extended for new business segments. Essentially, no part of the company was immune to transformation efforts.

In 1990, the freight mail division had annual losses of DM 2.2 billion. "The primary objective had to be to reduce costs and at the same time increase quality so that we could withstand the competition from other service providers on the market," said Deutsche Post CEO Zumwinkel. "To do so required the development of a new concept."

At the heart of this new concept were 33 completely new freight mail centers equipped with state-of-the-art technology. With this new transport and production concept, items were to be conveyed within a 24 or 48 hour timeframe with a guarantee that 80 percent of the items would reach the addressee on the day after they were posted. A detailed track and tracing system ensured the interplay of state-of-the-art processing and information technology. After an investment of DM 4.25 billion, the concept was fully implemented in July 1995, and has been functioning successfully. The change has been embraced by employees and the public alike. Due to the weak economic situation, it will take longer to reach a breakeven point.

In the letter mail service division, Deutsche Post had a prime objective to supply high quality by means of an efficient logistics system and to reduce costs. At the same time, it was very important in this sector to offer new products specially tailored to the customer's demands.

Taking these requirements into account, Deutsche Post began implementation of a new production process in conjunction with new transport works. Much of the preliminary logistical work necessary for this, as well as the successful introduction of five-digit post codes, has been completed. By the end of 1999, Deutsche Post hopes to process all of the letters in 83 letter mail centers with state-of-the-art technology.

While only in the implementation stage of this initiative, the quality of letter delivery times has improved. For example, over one year, the speed of delivery has increased from 83 percent to 90 percent of letters being delivered on the day after posting.

Deutsche Post also recognized that its retail outlet network had to be optimized. As in the other postal divisions, the same objectives applied: increase quality, reduce costs. Another objective — which also was a tactic in achieving overall objectives — was the use of new sales channels which Deutsche Post had never before tried.

The characteristics of the retail outlet network gave an indication of the problem: although Deutsche Post had the largest network of retail outlets in Germany, their revenues barely covered 50 percent of their annual cost to operate.

To remedy this situation, Deutsche Post embarked on a broad optimization program. Seventy new service outlets were opened by the end of 1995. By using the latest information technology and fitting the outlets with terminals, Deutsche Post not only facilitated the transactions, but also simplified the entire accounting process.

To further optimize the network, Deutsche Post closed down unprofitable outlets owned by the company. At the same time, in order to maintain a nationwide network, postal agencies were opened at promising locations in existing units — such as retailers, filling stations or kiosks. In comparison to company-owned outlets, these outlets are much less costly to maintain despite the same range of products and much longer business hours than their outlet predecessors.

### Integrating East German Postal Operations

Another considerable challenge for Deutsche Post during this period of internal transformation was the integration of the former East German postal operations. According to CEO Zumwinkel, "That came at a difficult time. We had just begun with strategic reorientation, with the development of new structures and the introduction of new systems. We only discovered on the spot just how obsolete conditions in Eastern Germany actually were. I think we achieved a lot in implementing this huge merger in the shortest possible time thanks to the courageous approach we took, the heavy investments we made and to the commitment shown by our staff." Despite enormous productivity and quality problems, Deutsche Post has succeeded in bringing the services rendered in eastern Germany up to the high standard of those rendered in western Germany within a short space of time. However, as Dr. Zumwinkel admits, "The high structural deficits which we inherited are still weighing our company down to this present day."

**Germany's New Business Focus and Plans for the Future**

The German post's transformation has been driven by the recognition that quality had to be improved across the entire organization. "Quality is a major concern of management, which strongly supports change initiatives," says Klaus Zumwinkel. "We recognized that the basis for lasting competitiveness could only be created if the entire company underwent a far-reaching, strategic reorientation process focused on quality."

In the sales outlets, quality teams have been assembled to ensure customer-oriented changes are implemented quickly. Deutsche Post has been careful to directly involve staff members in these quality teams and to take staff members' opinions very seriously. Test customers and customer surveys routinely give precise information on the extent to which noticeable improvements have taken effect for the customers.

Total Quality Management is being set up in the letter mail division. External delivery-time measurement systems ensure that success is monitored constantly. Additionally, quality teams are on site in the letter mail centers to ensure continuous improvement of the production process.

Once Deutsche Post took the measures required in its core business, it turned its attention to opening up new business segments. As a goal, it targeted DM 4.9 billion sales in these new business segments by the year 2000. The strategy was to accomplish this through an extension of infrastructure and supplementation of core businesses.

For example, the letter mail business has been successfully supplemented by in-house mail services. In this instance, Deutsche Post is successfully handling the mail of a number of large companies on an outsourced basis. It also created PostDirekt, which is a special offer for advertisers where Deutsche Post deals with their direct mailings from start to finish.

In the freight sector, Deutsche Post introduced "Contract-logistics." This service is intended to offer customers total solution packages in the future, which will include, as examples, warehousing, order-picking and call centers.

Deutsche Post also recognized the importance of electronic transmission technologies. It entered into this business segment with ePOST. This service allows customers to transmit their items to a post by means of a diskette or data link. The post then converts the items into hard copy, places them in envelopes, distributes and delivers them to the customers.

Deutsche Post is currently working with International Data Post to ensure that ePOST can be used globally by developing a uniform technological standard for the electronic mail service. At present there are already 13 countries including the United States, which are interconnected within the ePOST system. Customers — especially those large-volume mailers needing a fast, secure, reliable way to send mail such as invoices, orders or account statements between Germany and the other gateway countries — will have a global reach for messages needing guaranteed security.

And Deutsche Post is letting innovation open up new organizational paths. It formed "virtual companies" for the individual business sectors. These companies can act like small, independent enterprises. They are managed by "managing directors" and are independent of the usual decision-making processes within Deutsche Post. However, project progress is monitored by supervisory boards composed of top managers from the company.

## Germany's Structural Transformation Mastered

The obvious business success achieved over the past five years has been based on the consistent strategic reorientation of the entire company. "Postal Reform I created opportunities for the postal service to operate in the market by and large autonomously," says Dr. Zumwinkel, "and the company successfully seized these opportunities because we took a textbook approach in everything we did. To begin with, the new management engaged in a systematic stocktaking. In other words it intentionally wanted to reveal the strength and weakness of the company and to identify the opportunities and threats which exist on postal markets."

As for Deutsche Post's performance since corporatization, Dr. Zumwinkel observes, "First of all, we have greatly improved quality standards in all business divisions. The letter mail service has achieved quality metrics in excess of 90 percent and 99 percent as regards speed and reliability. Secondly, the improved financial situation of the company is naturally a very important result of the programs launched. Since Postal Reform I, revenue has improved by almost 50 percent. And we have succeeded in continuously increasing the result generated from ordinary business over the past five years. Above all, however, significant steps have been taken in the direction of creating a market- and customer-oriented company. And, true to our motto, 'We are getting better every day.'"

| | Denmark (1995) |
|---|---|
| 1995 GDP (US $ Billions) | 137 |
| 1994 Population (millions) | 5.2 |
| Owner | Government |
| 1995 stamp cost (US$) | 59 cents |
| Employees | 25,027 |
| Revenue (US $ billions) | 1.5 |

**DENMARK**

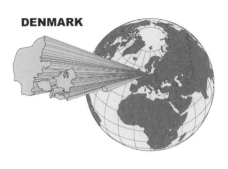

## Post Danmark — Transforming "Business as Usual"

Denmark's postal sector recently experienced legislative reform that opens the way for monopoly deregulation and fosters a commercial outlook at the postal administration. Passed in 1995, the Postal Activities Act could potentially open the monopoly as it gives the minister responsible for postal matters the authority to alter the reserved — or monopoly — area, including the authority to remove the monopoly in international mail.

Another 1995 bill, the Post Danmark Act, officially transformed Denmark's post from a government department to a semi-autonomous corporation fully owned by the government. Renamed Post Danmark, the post has greater flexibility and an unambiguous commercial mandate. The new organization reports directly to the government's Board of Trade and Industry and assumes its own liability.

The new enterprise is driven by three strategic goals designed to result in operational improvements to reduce production costs; to increase customer orientation; and to improve quality to maintain competitiveness and to fulfill its social obligation in connection with the exclusive rights given to Post Danmark.

These strategic goals were applied to Post Danmark's operations across-the-board. As was the case with Deutsche Post, no aspect of its operations was immune to the transformation effort.

Post Danmark recognized that, as the number of traditional paper-based services offered in its counters business area declines, the need to reduce fixed costs increases. Consequently, it decided on a strategic change in order to clear the hurdles to change. Its one-sided rationalization efforts were replaced by a dual strategy, ensuring adjustment of the counters business through a dialogue with the local communities which allowed a local shop or store to take over postal services. This move also helped establish a development concept for the counters business. This has led within a surprisingly short time to a number of service innovations — establishment of bank activities at post offices, development of financial services, sales of train tickets and tickets for sports and cultural events, among them. At the same time a large number of smaller post offices were converted into post shops with the approval of the local community. Said Helge Israelsen, Managing Director of Post Danmark, "In connection with adjustment of the counters business, we chose communications based on dialogues rather than our previous, more aggressive approach. It's paid off."

Because competition from electronic media increasingly threatens traditional mail, Post Danmark began to focus on creating new added-value products for customers. Strategically, this meant that Post Danmark needed to focus on the customers' value chain and development of a total solution for the customers, including communication, distribution and logistics. "The addressed letter is considered a warm media, and as a sales tool it will always have its place. We must assist with segmentation of customer groups, and handle responses to inquiries, stockholding, delivery of mail and transfer of payments," observed Israelsen.

Early on in the transformation process, Post Danmark conceded that the prevailing attitude was that distribution was typically a "one man's job" with "every man having his own route." The system was very inflexible, not business-oriented and driven in large part by administration and work agreements.

Beginning in 1990, delivery has been carried out with production groups as the supporting organizational structure. Within two years, this resulted in a productivity improvement of 20 percent in distribution service as employees grew more willing to adjust to the tasks to be performed. Each postal area receives a fixed budget based on the number of households in the postal area, and on a prognosis on the quantity of mail to be delivered. The budget sum is distributed to the production groups, which are afforded considerable independence in controlling day-to-day manpower that corresponds to the tasks required. "We are currently negotiating with the personnel organizations regarding implementation of wages based on results, rewarding good quality, effective consumption of material and improvements in methods. This will considerably strengthen the competitiveness of the company," stated Israelsen.

## Denmark's New Focus and Strategy

Development of a customer-oriented business culture has been a very high priority for Post Danmark. "Our local business process reengineering project — Business Focus — is based on a thorough analysis of what the customer will expect in the future with a lot of local influence on how business procedures can be simplified. The challenge for top management is to handle processes which are decided locally in order that implementation will have maximum impact," said Israelsen.

Post Danmark has also fully grasped the power of information technology and its implications for the post's future. The business is applying technology to both make production cheaper through automation and to offer customers more advanced, value-added solutions. Technology makes it possible to offer more sophisticated marketing to the customers than previously while information technology facilitates production. "Our efforts are designed to make it easier to trace quality problems and also plan work properly. We see the new technology as a strategic asset, which will help maintain jobs instead of eliminating them," explained Israelsen.

## Vision for the Year 2000

As it faces its future, Post Danmark has set a number of objectives. It has taken the position that future development possibilities will be ensured through improvement of the financial position of the company. Its target: net results before tax must be no less than 10 percent of revenue.

In its position as the preferred provider of printed communication, parcels and light goods in the market, Post Danmark intends to expand its presence by offering postal and distribution services which are competitive in terms of service, prices and quality. In turn, Post Danmark will strengthen the competitiveness of its customers by being a dependable, efficient and flexible distributor which creates added value in Denmark and in selected international markets through improvement of the customers' communications and the exchange of goods with their customers.

Post Danmark has determined that electronic services offer great opportunities for the future. In fact, the relatively high level of development of the electronic services marketplace in Denmark and the strong government support for information and communications technology suggests that electronic communication could form a serious threat to letter volumes sooner in Denmark than in other European countries. There could also be increased opportunities for new or additional revenue streams from electronic services.

Info Society 2000, a recent government report on the future of information and communications in Denmark, illustrates both the current high acceptance of communications technologies, as well as its implications. It is the government's position that personal computers will be present in 75 percent of households by 2000; that electronic access to public documents will be available; that there will be increased freedom for communications operators to offer interactive services and other commercial activities, either alone or in joint-venture with other distributors and producers; and that — in the future — all Danish companies will be connected by an electronic network.

Post Danmark has therefore positioned itself for participation in the electronic services marketplace to fit with overall strategic objectives, with an emphasis on developing and expanding new delivery mechanisms. One area on which it is focusing is direct marketing and mail order services.

## Danish Media Centers

Post Danmark believes that the development of services for media and mail order customers could play a significant role in replacing revenues lost due to falling letter volumes. Post Danmark currently offers a number of services for media/mail order customers as well as delivery of letters and parcels, although most of these services are on a very small scale. Media centers are designed to provide a way of coordinating and extending Post Danmark's mail order and direct marketing services externally to the customer while internally bringing together the post's media expertise and contacts.

Post Danmark believes the Media Center concept allows it to focus resources on serving specific customer groups of key importance in line with its overall strategy. The centers will provide a valuable sales support function by being the internal contact point for all questions on media services; provide specialist sales staff when necessary to accompany local sales and account representatives or to follow up on leads; and provide ongoing sales staff training. As planned, the centers will create an external perception of a center of excellence by raising Post Danmark's profile with customers as a result of the above initiatives. They'll avoid duplication of effort by co-locating hybrid mail and database management functions. The centers will act as an access channel to media buyers to increase the popularity of direct marketing by building up a knowledge base about all forms of media access to the consumer (including TV, radio and press), and by increasing contacts with media buyers to raise the profile of the postal service as a medium. Finally, the centers will help in developing marketing initiatives to support the sale of new products and services.

Post Danmark estimates that there are about 115,000 companies in Denmark who might potentially use direct mail to target their customers. These companies cover a wide spectrum of businesses from agriculture and forestry to manufacturing to financial services. Approximately 65,000 of these companies already use direct mail (although only a third do so to any great extent) and the post estimates that a further 50,000 companies may be interested in raising their profile in this way.

Post Danmark intends to offer a complementary service to Media Centers for smaller customers (less than five employees) not targeted by local sales forces. Operating in individual post offices, the mail shop would offer advisory services, for example, on setting up a database or using direct marketing to customers.

| | Malaysia |
|---|---|
| 1995 GDP (US $ Billions) | 87 |
| 1994 Population (millions) | 20.7 |
| Owner | Government |
| 1995 stamp cost (US$) | 12 cents |
| Employees | 11,914 |
| Revenue (US $ billions) | 11.5 |

## Pos Malaysia — Achieving its Vision for Postal Transformation

At Coopers & Lybrand's 1995 International Postal Forum, Tan Sri Zainol Mahmood, executive chairman of Pos Malaysia Berhad, stated, "All the Malaysian energy and efforts are being coordinated and harnessed to achieve our national vision 2020. That is, by the year 2020 we are determined to become a fully developed and industrialized country in all aspects — economically, politically, spiritually, psychologically and culturally." That might have sounded overly ambitious, but the facts indicate Malaysia is moving quickly and successfully in pursuit of its vision.

Malaysia, population just over 20 million, has emerged as the fastest-developing nation in the world's most economically dynamic region. In Kuala Lumpur, the world's tallest building is under construction, joining an already impressive number of other skyscrapers. Forty-five minutes away, what will be one of the world's largest airports is being built. When it's completed, it will be linked to the city center by a high speed rail system rivaling those in Japan and France. Coupled with an entirely new, ultra-modern 19.9 billion Ringgit (U.S.

$8 billion) capital city being built at Putra Kaya and work on one of Asia's largest dams, Malaysia is hurtling into the future.

While the terrain of Malaysia's infrastructure undergoes continuous development, so too has Pos Malaysia. The genesis of Malaysia's dramatic transformation lies in the privatization policy, "Vision 2020," a bold, forward looking program announced in 1983. Vision 2020 encourages and facilitates private sector participation in the development of the country as a developed nation by the year 2020. With an annual growth rate of eight percent or better, it may well achieve that goal. Several sectors of the economy have been privatized since the inception of the privatization program, including power, telecommunications, highways, ports and airports.

Pos Malaysia was corporatized as a public limited company in 1992, with the government transferring most of its assets and all liabilities to the new company. The original objectives of the corporatization were to relieve the financial and administrative burden of the government; to improve efficiency and productivity; to facilitate economic growth; to reduce the size and presence of the public sector in the economy; and to assist in meeting the national development targets.

"Pos Malaysia woke up one bright tropical morning in July 1994 and decided to modernize itself," said Tan Sri Zainol Mahmood. "We set ourselves the target of turning Pos Malaysia into the most modern postal industry in the whole region within two years."

To initiate its transformation, Pos Malaysia gradually implemented throughout the country an overall review and modernized delivery operation. Improvements were made on a broadly three-pronged strategy: restructuring of work methods, introduction of various operational controls and upgrading of physical facilities.

Records of addresses and points of call are the basis of a good delivery system — which Malaysia lacked. Accordingly, substantial areas of the country were surveyed. Addresses were identified as to type — business or residential — and recorded with route maps. A computerized route organization system was produced. The system helps in the proper allocation of postmen to beats. It also determines equitability of workload and ultimately measures the effectiveness of postmen and delivery branches.

Delivery operations were streamlined. Primary sorting was moved to mail centers. Mail is now being fine sorted and dispatched to delivery in containerized trays. This new work arrangement derives benefits in achieving service performance standards. It also is designed for the eventual efficient use of mechanized letter sorting systems including the current introduction of optical character reading machines.

Existing physical facilities were reviewed in order to adapt to new operational and delivery function strategies. The strategy was to consolidate mail operations to a reduced number of sites. New and spacious sites were established and existing sites were refurbished. A program was developed to introduce and gradually expand the use of containers to transport mail between centers. Transport facilities were also upgraded. While containerizing and upgrading of transport systems led to increased costs, they were offset by savings in operational costs.

Sorting frames were replaced by newly designed sorting equipment designed to align the mail exactly in the order of delivery. It obviates the necessity of two sorts: first to break the mail into 'groups' of streets and secondly into each group of delivery points.

## Transforming Malaysia's Processing, Operations and Delivery

Pos Malaysia set itself two clear objectives in the modernization of mail processing. The first was to achieve a reliable and consistent service performance of 98 percent on time delivery by July 31, 1996. The second was to reduce operational costs.

For years, the mail processing had been treated as a routine process, rather than being managed as a business. There were no structured systems in place to enable management to gain control and effectively monitor the performance of the mail processing function. The challenge was to introduce the idea of "end to end" management of operations where activities are seen as part of a complete process, rather than isolated, independent action. Ujimel, a mail-volume monitoring system, was designed to meet that challenge.

Pos Malaysia modernized its mail processing by introducing a production system based on factory production principles. The key feature of the system is matching the resource with the volume by managing the numbers. Supervisors use process control sheets as a monitoring tool to record the labor hours used, the volume processed and the unproductive hours. The data collected by the supervisors is entered into the computer daily to generate the production report which highlights the key performance indicators of the mailroom such as the number of man-hours used, volume processed and unprocessed, productivity, unproductive hours, overtime hours and absenteeism level. By referring to the report, the mail center manager can easily observe and assess the daily performance of his center.

The historical data stored in the computer helps the production planner to forecast and plan in advance on a weekly basis the man-hours required to process the mail. This planning tool also is used in scheduling workers' annual vacations.

This process of collecting the data, generating the report, producing the plan and implementing is known as the Production Cycle. The objective in using the systems is to ensure the allocation of the right number of resources to process the volume received at the right time.

The project's success can be measured in several ways. First, it met its July 31, 1996 target of 98 percent on time delivery, which is among the best in the world (see Figure 6-1). Second, its customers are receiving this modernized efficient service at a per-letter rate that is among the lowest in the world.

Another success of the project is its acceptance by Pos Malaysia workers. "People within our operation are communicating with each other using new terms that they never used before. Terms such as clear floor, carryover, productivity, target time, down time and end to end process. Managers are managing mail processing as a business by using data and, at the same time, asking the right questions and providing the right answers," explained the Malaysian post's executive chairman last year.

Pos Malaysia also undertook a modernization of its finance and management information systems. The objectives of the efforts were to generate management information that enables mail operation managers to manage by numbers; and instill greater financial accountability.

Prior to modernization efforts, information key to managing an effective mail operation was localized in nature, generated by certain groups or individuals to try to manage their own work area. Consequently, it was difficult to extract key information for use by other managers or for presentation to management.

Figure 6-1

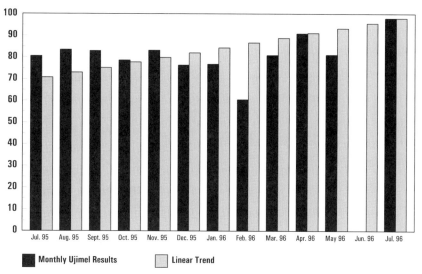

Pos Malaysia's On-Time Delivery

■ Monthly Ujimel Results    ▢ Linear Trend

To help management manage day-to-day operations, a number of systems were installed. The mail volume monitoring system receives daily data on the volume and type of mail processed (franked, bulk, registered, or air), consolidated in a monthly report. This system enables managers to use the information to plan and managed the operational side of the business. The Ujimel system samples, on a daily basis, one in 20 letters recorded at selected delivery offices. The daily results are updated into the Ujimel system at corporate headquarters. This system indicates the service performance with and end to end view of the mail operations. Mail operation managers use this information, plus other key mail operation reports, to improve the mail service performance. Key performance indicator boards have been installed in 14 locations. All key information pertaining to main operations, including cost and manpower data, are recorded on a daily, weekly and monthly basis.

Completion and submission via fax of state daily operating reports to the corporate headquarters forms another mandatory requirement for monitoring Pos Malaysia's daily mail operations. The data reports on the last 24 hours' activities for delivery, processing and transport. Each day, state managers from each of the country's 14 states teleconference to discuss the state daily operating report on the previous day's operations. Finally, an employee database system provides managers access to reports pertaining to manpower and manpower cost. This gives managers the tools to effectively muster the necessary resources to meet mail volume in light of cost implications.

The results of these efforts are apparent. While Pos Malaysia mail operation managers are still acclimating themselves to using information technology of this type and complexity, these systems have made a clear difference in performance.

Transport activity plays a key role in the success of the end-to-end mail process, providing the linkage for the flow of mail products between mail centers and customers. An efficient transport system capable of providing maximum processing windows and consistently achieving high performance in meeting target transport schedules plays a very significant role in contributing to the achievement of a high mail service standard.

Pos Malaysia's transport set-up and systems during pre-modernization days were lacking in business focus, used inadequate monitoring and controls and suffered from weak coordination between headquarters and regional transport units. Transport activities also incurred high overtime costs, lacked a sense of urgency and were characterized by incompatible vehicle specifications and equipment as well as the absence of clear job descriptions.

The solution, Pos Malaysia determined, was to implement modern transport principles and operational systems while maximizing vehicle utilization, containerization, "right" vehicle specifications and configuration.

The strategy adopted to achieve this was one of staff involvement at all levels; managing by numbers; and providing on-the-job training to encourage staff acceptance of higher productivity targets, cost reductions and other changes in work methods. "This approach has worked," said Tan Sri Zainol Mahmood. "The positive response from the staff led to greater cooperation and understanding, which resulted in a smoother transition and a greater sense of ownership of the new system."

The Pos Malaysian chief executive added that managing by numbers has also helped the managers understand how performance levels are measured and what they can do to improving them. "Our job training has succeeded in teaching us to work smarter and in a more systematic and efficient manner," he observed.

Its efforts to improve its line haul transport performance have proven successful. The unit has achieved a consistent 94-to-95 percent on-time delivery record while maintaining a low cost-per-kilogram of mail product transported. Transport staff are also showing a greater sense of urgency and accountability in carrying out their daily tasks. "This work culture, together with effective systems and controls and the now institutionalized concept of managing by the numbers, has greatly strengthened our transport organization. We have much better control of the operation and that's why we can deliver the type of performance expected of a modernized transport structure," said Tan Sri Zainol Mahmood.

"By 12 midnight on 31 July 1996, our standard of service should reach 98 percent, which is among the best in the world. Our mail service will not only be efficient and reliable, but consistently efficient and reliable. Our customers will enjoy the most modern, reliable and efficient service, at the same rate, which is at 7.5 pence (US $.12) per letter, among the lowest in the world," the Malaysian chief executive concluded.

## Conclusion

Germany, Denmark and Malaysia have successfully corporatized their postal services — though the manner and speed in which they did so is strikingly different. The experience of the postal administration of these three countries serve as excellent examples of how a "one size fits all" approach would fail to take into account the particular circumstances and challenges of different posts. In any case, these three postal services stand poised to move into the next phase of transformation — divestiture — when and if they determine the need to.

# Chapter

# 7

## TRANSFORMATION'S FINAL PHASE— DIVESTITURE

*"The blind, unplanned, uncoordinated wisdom of the market is overwhelmingly superior to the well-researched, rational, systematic, well-meaning, co-operative, science-based, forward-looking, statistically respectable plans of governments, bureaucracies and international organizations."*
— Sir Keith Joseph, United Kingdom

As the world's economies are driven by forces of change, governments in Europe, Asia and South America have been pushed to reexamine their roles in the provision of public services. Purse strings are being tightened as the gap increases between what these nations are asked for and are able to provide. In addition to global competition, politicians are being faced with increasing demands from their constituents. The voters expect public services to equal or exceed what they routinely receive from the private sector.

In fact, research indicates that during this decade, privatization has become a key objective for governments around the world for the improved performance that the process brings. "Driven by the realization that markets succeed only when private markets and efficiencies are allowed to bloom," observed Henrietta Holsman Fore of the US Agency for International Development, "privatization is now sweeping the world." That was four years ago. So widespread is this acceptance that in 1996, the value of privatizations worldwide reached an all-time record of over $85 billion, beating the previous record achieved in 1995 of almost $74 billion.

This growth trend certainly supports a broadening consensus that, as the late Sir Keith Joseph, a former United Kingdom cabinet minister, sagely observed twenty years ago, the unfettered nature of a free market is a vastly better business environment than any carefully planned by a government.

While international powers such as Germany, the United Kingdom, Italy and Japan topped the 1996 list of total funds raised, privatization has extended beyond the developed countries that pioneered it to the developing world. The extent to which privatization has become a global phenomenon is illustrated by a recent study that reveals that nearly one-third of the privatizations taking place last year are in countries outside the OECD — $25 billion out of a total of $85 billion. One of the effects of the spread of privatization to the non-OECD countries will be to narrow the gap between the developed and the developing world. While not all privatizations are successful, when they are, they deliver significantly better performance. That, plus the side effect of stimulating savings and local capital markets, will tend to improve the performance of developing countries' economies.

A recent International Finance Corporation study of the impact of privatization claims that in over 70 percent of the privatizations in which it has been involved, there have been clear economic benefits. In Chile, the transfer to private ownership has resulted in the doubling of the telephone network in four years; in Argentina, railroad subsidies were sharply reduced following privatization; export earnings increased in Poland; and the Czech Republic and Egypt enjoyed a widened range of banking services.

Today, the privatization process, which has been carried out the most thoroughly and for the past 17 years in the United Kingdom, goes beyond the sale of public assets. It also involves a fundamental reappraisal and reinvigoration of the way organizations are run. The process moves from entities which were part of bureaucratic government departments through a process of commercialization, corporatization, and finally into the private sector — facing the full force of competition. "Firms such as British Airways, British Telecom and British Steel have turned from corporate dogs into some of the world's most admired companies," concluded one report in the *Economist* magazine.

Those lessons learned in the UK have been applied overseas. In the telecommunications industry, Spain's sale of Argentaria and Germany's sale of Deutsch

Telekom followed the British Telecom approach. Australia's second Commonwealth Bank share sale, or *flotation*, had many features in common with similar sales in England, and France adopted the English technique of issuing "bonus shares" to promote wider ownership after an initial sale.

As a consequence, the debate has moved beyond the question, "Why privatize?" to how best to accomplish even wider private sector involvement in public service provision. Understanding where this debate is going is helpful in anticipating the evolution of postal privatization worldwide, and to anticipate the response of public sectors to market forces.

## Postal Divestiture — Different Paths, Same Destination

In postal and all industries, divestiture is the sale to the private sector of either the whole or part of a governments' shareholding in an enterprise. In little more than a decade, the one-time unthinkable loss of state control over strategic assets has been replaced by an acceptance by policy-makers of the improved performance that private ownership brings.

For most countries' postal administrations, however, the path to divestiture is too difficult a journey to complete at present. Marketplace rules, regulatory inhibitors, aggrieved (sometimes legitimately, sometimes not) constituents all pose tall hurdles for postal administrations or governments to leap to achieve full privatization. In the Netherlands, the privatization of PTT Post followed a national economic upheaval that underscored the need for industry change. Major economic reform is driving events in Argentina. In move stable economics, privatization of the postal industry may not be just around the corner. As United States

Postmaster General Marvin Runyon noted in an interview with us, "I don't think private sector delivery of the mail is the right way to go. America's mail provider should be accountable to the federal government. The ultimate answer is corporatization — a communications business owned by the American people." Some world postal leaders, however, see privatization as a long range inevitability. In this chapter, we will examine how organizations prepare for divestiture as a private company. This process is well established in some sectors — such as telecommunications and utilities — and is gaining momentum in the postal sector.

There are a number of reasons why privatization-through-divestiture as a means of public sector restructuring is now economic orthodoxy worldwide. It can meet a wide variety of government and public objectives. It frees an enterprise from the constraints of public control. It relieves the economy from the burden of public subsidy and deficit. It attracts capital, including foreign investment. It acts as a stimulant to both efficient business and to effective government.

Among a number of major government privatization initiatives, China is working to restructure the China National Petroleum Corporation, the fifth largest producer of crude oil in the world, to meet competitive market conditions. In Germany, the Treuhandanstalt, which was set up after the country's unification and is the world's largest holding company, is addressing the massive task of privatizing approximately 13,000 enterprises employing over four million people. Mexico is in the process of restructuring the Mexican Railroad. Argentina has privatized over 80 percent of the public sector since 1990. And, as we will see later, British Telecom represents a significant achievement of the part of the British government to successfully divest a major public enterprise.

Careful planning is needed to apply the right method of privatization for the desired objective. Very different conditions may apply in different political systems, but success for a privatization program should normally be seen in terms of achieving better products and services at a lower cost, rather than merely winning one-off injections of cash for governments. However, a successful privatization often can be expected to generate a significant up-side for the treasury, both in the form of cash for selling the business and in increased tax revenue from the more profitable business being formed. This potential financial gain, however, must be weighed against postal's societal obligations to the general public and business community.

While it can be relatively easy to sell or privatize a company, it is more important that the government's objectives for the sale are met. A crucial step is to identify those objectives properly. They are likely to vary depending on the country and the industry, and they may also turn out to be contradictory in effect: for instance, achieving the highest sales price can be incompatible with maximizing the benefits to the customer, or achieving wider share ownership.

Establishing the government's objectives is made more complex by the multiple roles it must play. Often there are different government departments involved in the debate, each with different goals. In essence, the government must reconcile its responsibilities as shareholder, regulator and banker, while fulfilling its societal obligations for the delivery of mail. The key is to balance objectives to ensure as far as possible that all parties share fairly in the future benefits.

Once the government's objectives and approach to privatization are agreed to, the enterprise must be prepared. Where a direct sale is involved, the business will have to be valued. A regulatory strategy may need to be determined to contain postal obligations, monopoly powers and broader service objectives. Legislation must be drafted and the capital structure put in place. Other alternatives, such as joint ventures or management contracts, will be appropriate depending upon the circumstances and differing requirements for success.

Where a sale is involved, implementation requires agreement on the appropriate form. For example, Peru is clustering together — for a sale to a group of investors — seven mines and a metallurgical complex, which also has four hydroelectric plants, houses, a hospital, schools, shops and a television station. By contrast, Western European governments have tended to privatize larger entities by way of public flotations. In these cases, extensive knowledge of international capital markets is absolutely essential for success.

Partnerships, franchising and privatization approaches vary widely. The Netherlands Post, for example, is part of a group called KPN, which also includes the telephone company, and which is majority owned by the private sector. Singapore Post, as part of Singapore Telecom, is also partly owned by the public. Argentina has privatization plans in progress which include the letting of a concession to run the national postal service for several decades. Others have carried corporatization and profitability to the point that privatization may be a feasible next step in commercialization. For example, in the UK, the debate continues on whether to privatize Royal Mail and Parcelforce, two of the UK Post Office's four lines of business. Many other national posts are widely contracting for services in the areas of retail franchising, contract transportation, delivery to remote areas, information technology services and business partnerships for certain products.

### Working Through the Process

The final step of divesting to the private sector all or part of a government's shareholding in an enterprise can take many forms. In some instances it may be a two-step process: in the Netherlands, for instance, the government sold a minority stake during phase one, and following a second offering, effectively became a private company. Generally speaking, divestitures usually take one of the following forms: public flotation, private sales or management buy-outs.

*Public flotation* is the public offering of shares based on a prospectus. The floated company is listed and its shares are quoted on the stock market. Of the three forms of divestiture, public flotation reaches the widest range of private investors and institutions but demands the most preparation and marketing. The government, with the help of professional advisors, has to prepare a prospectus to provide essential information to potential shareholders, as well as market the offer vigorously to ensure that it reaches all interested parties.

*Private sales* can be done in two ways: private placements with institutional investors or a group of interested parties; and trade sales to other private sector companies. A private placement with interested parties may take the form of a sale to a consortium of commercial companies, one of which takes responsibility for managing the enterprise. The outcome is typically some form of a joint venture. A trade or treaty sale is a direct sale to a corporate entity. The process may entail a negotiated sale with one potential buyer, or a tender with a number of bidders. The sale is usually based on an information memorandum which is similar in content to, but often less detailed than, a public prospectus. The process is less demanding for the seller than a public flotation because the buying company is able to conduct its own investigation of the acquired business before completing the purchase.

*Management buy-outs* (MBOs) result in the managers of the enterprise acquiring control of the assets of the business. Such buy-outs are invariably highly leveraged and the assets acquired are used as security to borrow a large part of the purchase price. On occasion, employees as well as managers take shares in the buyout. MBOs are sometimes followed by a public flotation to enable the original buyers to realize part or all of their capital and/or to reduce leveraging.

The form that a particular divestiture takes will depend on several factors: the capacity and state of the capital markets; the attitude of the capital markets and potential shareholders to the enterprise; past profitability of the enterprise and its prospects; competitiveness of the market within which the enterprise operates; and the proportion of the enterprise that is to be sold.

## Choosing What Form a Divestiture Should Take

Although Argentina is entertaining privatization through a concession contract that would allow an operator to run its national post for decades and capture the profits — or absorb the losses — of such a venture, this approach is not the norm. Rather, the sale of shares is more often the route chosen.

For a public flotation to succeed, two conditions must apply. First, the capital market needs to be well enough developed to absorb the offer of shares: some capital markets do not yet have that capacity and, where capacity does exist, market volatility may be a problem. Secondly, the enterprise needs to be attractive to potential investors: usually that means that it should have a record of profitability and good prospects of maintaining it. In the absence of either condition, public flotation can be highly risky. This implies for less developed postal services, trade sales or concessions will be appropriate, but for the larger or more advanced services, public flotations will be possible.

Public flotations give governments the opportunity both to widen and to deepen the capital market by bringing in new shareholders and new money. The United Kingdom has been very successful in widening the market, attracting millions of first-time equity investors through massive advertising, attractive sales prices and bonuses, and weighting the allocation of shares in oversubscribed offers in favor of smaller shareholders. Desirable, too, is the ability for employees to own part of the business and feel more responsible for its performance. Wider ownership has, however, been attained only at significant cost to the state treasury in revenue forgone in pricing the offers, in substantial marketing and in the costs of supervising large public offerings to ensure a fair allocation and guard against fraudulent applications.

To ease a capital market constraint on the scale of a public flotation, the immediate impact of the offer of shares can be reduced by selling the equity of the company in tranches and issuing part paid shares, the balance of the issue price to be paid by the investor in one or more installments at a later date.

Trade sales and MBOs have been used widely to dispose of parts of larger public enterprises and to divest enterprises whose short record of profitability or uncertain future would make them unattractive to the wider public.

Trade sales are often the easiest and quickest method of divestiture. But a number of factors need to be weighed up before an offer for sale is made. The key questions are:

- Is the price reasonable? A tender with many bidders may suggest that the sale price is reasonable; in many cases, however, there may be few bidders, or only one. If the sale is a large one, the number of potential bidders attracted may be increased by adopting deferred or lease purchase to reduce the initial capital outlay.
- What strings are attached? Bidders may request warranties from the government — particularly if the government is an important supplier or buyer for the company. Otherwise, bidders in some countries may seek tax concessions or policy incentives. Such requests need to be evaluated with the price offers in assessing alternative bids.
- What will be the effect on competition? Often, the most interested bidders are companies in the same or a related line of business. To maintain effective competition and avoid the formation of dominant companies, some companies may need to be excluded from bidding (even if they might have offered the highest price). In countries with small private corporate sectors, trade sales may result in an undesirable concentration of power and wealth.
- What is the attitude to foreign ownership? Strategic interests may require the imposition of a limitation or special restrictive provisions on bids from foreign companies.

One of the bidders in a trade sale may well be the management team proposing an MBO. The special feature of an MBO is the direct stake it gives to a management team already knowledgeable about the enterprise and the resulting strong commitment of management to the success of the business. If the MBO includes widespread employee participation, the sense of commitment will increase.

MBOs have other potential advantages. They allow confidential discussions to be held between government (as shareholder) and the management (as potential purchaser), thereby removing some of the uncertainties which otherwise arise before the proposed sale is made public. They reduce the need for the public disclosure of confidential and competitively sensitive company information. They reduce the need for warranties from government because the managers know the business. And they lessen the risk of ownership passing into foreign control (at least until a later stage).

The first requirement for success of an MBO is an effective management team, willing and able to assemble an attractive funding package. Since few public sector managers have private wealth, most MBOs involve equity participation by financial institutions and high leveraging. The most suitable businesses for disposal are those with a strong cash flow and sound asset base that do not require excessive new investment in the short term. If these features are not present, the government needs to be willing to sell the assets at a much discounted price to compensate for the inherent risk.

**Should Government Retain a Shareholding?**

The Dutch government privatized the postal service, PTT Post, in two public offerings that resulted in over 50 percent ownership of the holding company, KPN, by individuals or private institutions. With a clear commercial mandate from its stakeholders, PTT Post has become one of the most aggressive competitors in the international mail market, capturing market share from sister postal administrations through its own activities and via acquisitions. KPN has now signalled a bolder global strategy by acquiring the Australia-based TNT group.

In the UK, where the government's ultimate goal has usually been total divestiture, it has generally been reached in one step. Sometimes a large minority or small majority has been sold initially (e.g., in British Petroleum or British Telecom) either to test the market or to keep the size of the flotation manageable, with the remainder being sold later.

In the past, the privatization of utilities has given those businesses opportunity to grow their market positions through joint venture and acquisition — for example, many of the Regional Bell Operating Companies of the United States have joint-ventured with European telecoms and other European organizations to achieve an objective of the globalization of all parties' product offerings. Lack of funds and risk-averse governments have prevented postal administrations from setting up such ventures.

If government retains a large shareholding, it needs to make the reasons for so doing clear to potential investors. These reasons may include the wish to share, as an investor, in the profitability of the company, or to avoid swamping the market. If the reasons are not stated, and potential investors suspect that government will use its holding to exert influence over the company, some investors may lose interest. One possible solution which gives assurance against interference but allows government to derive continued financial benefits is to convert government's residual shareholding into non-voting shares.

The net financial benefits of privatization to the government depend partly on whether the enterprises perform better in the private sector than under public ownership. If they do, the government gains from increased tax revenues.

## What Pricing Methods are Used in Selling the Enterprise?

One conventional method for the sale of a public flotation is a fixed price offer. The alternative is a sale by tender. Fixed prices sales are easier to organize and easier for investors to understand. Far more difficult is selecting a price that ensures maximum proceeds to the government, attracts investors to buy all the shares, and is in line with the movement of other share prices over the period between the price announcement and the closure of the offer. The tendency is to pitch a fixed price offer low to avoid the embarrassment of undersubscription if the market falls. The tender method avoids the problem of fixing the right price, but it may discourage potential investors.

Mixed fixed price and tender offers combine some of the advantages of each method. The public is invited to bid for a proportion of the shares at a fixed price, and the rest of the shares are sold by tender.

Setting the right price is easiest if the company is already quoted on the stock exchange (for example, if a minority government shareholding is being sold). The next easiest case is if there are closely comparable quoted companies. Unique enterprises are difficult to price. In some cases, the price of such companies has been fixed primarily by reference to a judgment on the appropriate price/earnings ratio or dividend yield. But likely earnings growth also has to be taken into account, since this ultimately determines the trend in shareholder value.

Divestiture of loss-making enterprises is inherently more difficult than the sale of profitable ones, although by no means impossible. The most likely method of sale is a trade sale or an MBO. If the enterprise is loss-making, the buyer is likely to request special concessions. Before agreeing, government needs to decide whether to rehabilitate the enterprise before divestiture. In extreme cases, the right decision may be to liquidate the enterprise and sell the assets rather than try to sell it as a going concern.

## What is the Impact on Efficiency?

Whether divestiture always results in improved efficiency is difficult to say. Many efficiency gains would in principle be achievable even if ownership of the enterprise were retained in the public sector. But efficiency may well be increased further by divestiture.

The transfer of control to the private sector provides an environment for more effective management: it removes government interference in decisions on capital investment, pricing and other strategic or operational issues and provides freedom to attract and retain good management by offering higher pay and the ability to act decisively. Privatization often triggers radical change in the way the enterprise is structured and operated, with resulting improvements in efficiency and commercial purpose. It may also increase the commitment of management and employees to the success of the business, especially if many employees own shares. The process is likely to make it easier to attract high caliber managers into the business — which is extremely important because the quality of management is probably the single most important ingredient in efficiency improvement.

Comparisons of efficiency of public and private enterprises are, however, difficult. While privatization does not automatically improve efficiency, it may, with effective management, facilitate such improvements. Moreover, the prospect of achieving privatization can sometimes be as much a spur to increased efficiency as privatization. In the UK, for example, the profitability of Cable & Wireless and of the National Freight Corporation increased dramatically after privatization, partly because management was highly motivated and partly because new business opportunities were seized. Another example is the British Steel Corporation, which achieved a remarkable turnaround in preparing itself for flotation. While privatization may be the spur, however, change of ownership itself has not been a necessary precursor of significant efficiency gains.

Increased efficiency has frequently involved shedding employees to improve labor productivity. In many cases, enterprises have shed large numbers of employees, usually in the period immediately before privatization. The impact on the individuals is usually softened by severance payments or early retirement packages, but the impact on locations where closures have occurred can sometimes be severe and active measures need to be taken to attract new employment.

Although some critics would argue that the social consequences of rapid shedding of labor is sometimes too severe, public enterprises which are to be privatized cannot afford to be burdened with unnecessary costs. The social burden of redeployment must be borne by government and therefore any substantial shedding of labor is best achieved before divestiture. The process of rebuilding confidence and skills in the displaced labor force and redeploying it into productive new activity must be planned to minimize personal and communal disruption.

### Taking a Lesson from British Telecom

The background to the world's embracing of privatization begins with the Seventies' massive growth in Britain's public sector that led to huge investments in the provision and modernization of infrastructure, transport and utility services. At that time, government control and ownership was perceived to be the best model for rapid economic growth. But the reality proved otherwise. Many public enterprises became persistent loss leaders, a drain on public finance. The public concluded most government activities were inefficient. Productivity lagged and the UK competitive position, vis-à-vis European competitors, was threatened. When potential financial benefits from the receipts from public sales were also factored in, the privatization policy was launched.

Between 1979 and 1994, many major state-run enterprises were privatized: British Petroleum, British Aerospace, Associated British Ports, Jaguar, British Telecom, British Gas, British Airways, Rolls-Royce, British Airports Authority, British Steel, water and sewage companies, electricity generating and transmission companies, and, in 1994 — British Rail. Most happened during the 1980s, when the policy was embraced by the United Kingdom public as services improved and prices and fees were reduced. The public treasury benefited, too. By 1981, state ownership had cost British taxpayers £50 million (approximately $75 million) a week in subsidies; 15 years later, the same firms contribute £55 million (more than $80 million) a week in taxes. The phenomenon was in full bloom.

Not that it was, or is, problem-free. There is an implicit dilemma in any privatization: deregulation, while in the consumers' interest, can delay a privatization (a state of limbo while the market is deregulated and the entity prepares for competition). As a result, sale proceeds are often reduced because the entity will achieve lower profits in a deregulated rather than a monopoly market.

Critics of the privatization policy in Britain have seized on this dilemma, claiming that decisions are primarily made for the benefit of the British Treasury. In response the British government argues it has tried to introduce competition, and gives as examples the sales of separate entities in industries: for example, two generators of electricity, Powergen and National Power, were created from the old Central Electricity Generating Board. New competitors have also been licensed, like Mercury, to compete in the UK telecommunications market, and tough regulation (including of prices) has been introduced.

Nevertheless, the flotation of British Telecom in the autumn of 1984 provides a classic case study of the first successful divestiture of a major public sector entity in the United Kingdom — and can serve well as a model for transformation. All the difficulties that by now are regarded as routine were present, but for the first time and on an unprecedented scale.

"The initial plan was to sell on the stock market 51 percent of the ordinary shares of British Telecom for about 4 billion pounds — at the time by far the biggest public sale of shares of a privatized government entity anywhere in the world," recalled Ian Morfett, an executive responsible for their biggest transformation program. "But the problems faced by the UK government were enormous." British Telecom had been part of a civil service department until 1969, and a separate corporation in its own right since 1981, when serious preparation for sale finally began. At that point, it was a monopoly utility business, funded and controlled by the government.

The approach to divestiture required a management — generally with little or no experience in the private sector — to address different challenges it had not before faced. There had to be a reconsideration of profitability and quality of service to customers despite an asset base that was difficult to predict, given the rapid changes in technology that made forecasting unreliable at best.

The pressure for change in the years prior to flotation in November of 1984 were relentless. British Telecom restructured and reorganized itself and concentrated both within and by way of external recruitment on ensuring that it would have appropriate management competence for its new environment.

A measure of some of these changes was provided by the financial accounts. Together with its auditors, who were also the reporting accountants, each of the accounting policies had to reviewed and amendments made where appropriate. Two billion pounds were written off the value of fixed assets. Difficulties that had led to audit report qualifications were eradicated. The presentation of information in the accounts, which were to be used as the basis for selling the company, was brought up to private sector standards, both in terms of disclosure and speed of issue. Forecasting procedures were overhauled.

The government had in the meantime to determine whether it was divesting itself of a utility telephone business or of a growth telecommunications group, and provide the legal framework for doing so. Among other issues was the question of the monopoly and how to protect the public by regulation of prices. As part of the process, competition for the supply of equipment was introduced, and the monopoly over the telephone network broken. Regulation took the form of licenses administered by Office of Telecommunications; prices were controlled by formula tying increases to the retail price index (the UK price index for consumer goods).

The necessary legal framework governing the UK telecommunications industry was detailed in the 1984

Telecommunications Act, which established the basis for licensing of the sector. Under the Act, the Department of Trade and Industry, through the Secretary of State for Trade and Industry, became the controlling regulatory and supervisory body responsible for telecommunications in the UK. Primary responsibility for the granting of licenses for telecommunications systems was retained by the Secretary of State, although power to license systems may be delegated to the Director General of the regulatory Office of Telecommunications.

This institutional framework presented additional challenges for British Telecom, in that it grants control of a small number of regulatory functions to a government ministry (i.e., the Department of Trade and Industry) while reserving control of a major part of the regulatory function to be undertaken by an independent, non-ministerial, non-governmental department, the Office of Telecommunications.

Meanwhile, the merchant bankers grappled with whether the shares could be sold in such numbers. Early on the decision was taken that the issue would have to be spread across the world and launched on the same day in the UK, the United States, Canada, Japan and Switzerland. There was, until a late stage, nervousness in London and open skepticism in New York about whether it would be possible at all.

There was also the delicate issue of the price and the marketing. For the first time ever, a coordinated television advertising campaign was launched in the UK to encourage new small investors, supported by incentives — in particular, bonus shares or vouchers giving reductions against telephone bills. Generous terms for share purchase were offered to employees. Roadshows were held in the United States, Canada, Japan and Europe to inform and encourage foreign investors.

Collectively, all the parties involved — the government, the auditors and reporting accountants, the merchant bankers, and the lawyers — had to prepare the prospectuses which were used to sell the shares on all five stock exchanges across the world. This involved a year's work, consultation with the appropriate controlling bodies in each country and, for the first time in the UK, the issue of a simplified prospectus designed for the small investor.

The public flotation of British Telecom in 1984 signaled a new era. It was the largest flotation that had been attempted anywhere in the world. It was also the first public utility to be privatized in the UK, and special regulatory arrangements had to be made to control possible abuses of monopoly (or oligopoly) power and to maintain supply and service standards.

One of the most important — and largely unpredicted — lesson learned from the privatization of British Telecom was that a major public flotation of this kind, given heavy publicity, could attract wide interest and investment from the public and employees. The government came to see expanding share ownership not only as a means of reinforcing the popularity of privatization but also as a means of making it more difficult for opposing forces to reverse the trend. By 1986, "popular capitalism" had become one of the main stated objectives of further privatization.

**Post-Divestiture: BT's Advances and Its Future**

The competition lost little time in responding when British Telecom lost its network monopoly in 1984. Mercury opened a network service which they have built into a 15 percent market share while making significant inroads in the key business sector, particularly large financial companies in London. Additionally,

British Telecom has been joined in the UK by over 100 other licensed operators, ranging from long distance network carriers to local cable television operations.

Against this competitive backdrop, however, British Telecom has fared well. It has continued to grow revenues through a period when telecommunication prices have halved in real terms. Said Ian Morfett, who has been at the heart of their transformation process, "This record has been achieved in a number of ways, not the least of which was significant capital investment in modernizing BT's network and developing new products and services. To accomplish this, BT has addressed new issues related to faster product development cycles and expanded marketing needs. The cycle for new product development used to be five years, today it is three years, and we're working toward reducing the cycle further to one year.

"From a performance perspective, the experience of British Telecom demonstrates the need not just to make but to sustain efficiency improvements," continued Morfett. Referring to the postal industry, he observed, "Many of the technologies postals are facing are equally relevant to the telecom industry — e-mail, faxes, electronic funds transfer and so on. With these new technologies come new markets, new customers, new products and new entrants — all the elements of competition. It's our experience within telecommunications that the competition comes most strongly from the companies already in the industry rather than from new entrants. It will be interesting to see if that's equally true with postals."

## The Role of Regulation

In the face of privatization efforts, postal regulators can be expected to place as a top priority ensuring that postal services maintain their universal service obligation — the provision of uniform, affordable service to the general population. This is true whether or not a postal monopoly exists. Consequently, regulation may extend beyond safeguards against abuses of a monopoly position. Even where there is no monopoly, policymakers may perceive a need to protect the public interest in matters such as safety, security and environmental conservation. The issue is complex. The regulation must protect the consumer, but be flexible enough to avoid stifling either the initiative of management or the development of competition. It must also be simple and clear enough to enable potential investors to interpret its possible commercial impact on the finances of the company in which they propose to invest.

Post-privatization regulation in the postal sector — if telecommunications and other industries are valid benchmarks — is likely to include financial performance, level and quality of service, and pricing and trading practices. The appropriate extent of regulation depends on both the structure of the industry and its particular characteristics. The form of regulation chosen for an electricity industry, for example, will depend on whether there is one electricity company or many, and will be determined by special requirements such as security of supply.

There are two main forms of regulating financial performance. In the United States, controls are exercised over profits but these do not directly encourage efficiency and may encourage unnecessary investment. The UK government has developed an alternative method of regulation, based on controls over prices.

The approach is to link a group of tariffs to the increase in the retail price index (RPI) by means of a formula which allows increases in regulated tariffs at a prescribed rate, usually below the movement in prices as a whole. Most common are the "RPI-x" and "RPI-x+y" formulae. The factor "x" is designed to reduce price increases below the increase in RPI to encourage efficiency; the "y" factor is used to take into account increases in the long-run marginal cost of non-renewable resources.

The broad regulatory RPI-x formula has the advantage of simplicity but it can be abused. For example, it does not prevent cross-subsidy of services which may put certain user groups at a serious disadvantage. Furthermore, reliance on a single financial measure, even if it is coupled with broad service obligations, may give too little emphasis to the quality and reliability of service and responsiveness to customer needs at the expense of controlling prices. Experience suggests that a broader range of mutually reinforcing performance and quality-of-service indicators may be required.

**Getting It Done**

Many of the issues involved in preparing for divestiture are interrelated and objectives are sometimes in conflict. The desire to maximize the proceeds to government can conflict with the objective of extending share ownership and building up investors' confidence in the long-term future of the enterprise. Moving rapidly can conflict with the wish to introduce greater competition through the break-up of monopolies and/or the deregulation of markets. Management freedom may well be difficult to reconcile with the need for regulation.

Enterprises that lend themselves to rapid divestiture are profitable nationalized companies in attractive industries with good medium-term prospects. Private companies that have been nationalized because they were unprofitable are more difficult to divest unless profitability has been restored and sustained. Preparing enterprises that have always been in the public sector for divestiture takes time — sometimes several years. A program of divestiture may therefore include the rapid divestiture of certain operations and the preparation for sale of more complex operations later.

## Post-Privatization Support

Privatization activity does not end with the sale. The regulation of privately-owned monopolies, for example in the water industry and other utilities, needs to be closely monitored to ensure that customers obtain the benefits expected from privatization and that competition is allowed to develop properly. Management must not only help to establish the regulatory authority before privatization, it must also stay involved to ensure that regulations fulfill their aims by evolving over time to reflect the changing performance of the operators, the effects of technological progress and the advent of competition.

In some cases, significant changes to the business are made before privatization: the management structure is reorganized to focus on customers; the business is refinanced; new management systems are implemented. However, some or all of these changes are often delayed until after privatization. In either case, these changes are just the start of a continuing process as the business improves its performance to meet customers' needs.

Two postal administrations at different extremes in the divestiture phase — the Netherlands and Argentina — are examples of the opportunities, and obstacles, divestiture can pose. Their stories follow.

# Chapter

# 8

## THE NETHERLANDS AND ARGENTINA— TWO STUDIES IN PRIVATIZATION

*"How do we live up to expectations? It's control of your company, knowing what you're doing. You have to have some creativity (so) that your big growth areas can be fueled, and then you have to hope that these areas live up to the expectations of your investors."*
—Ad Scheepbouwer, President, PTT Post (The Netherlands)

For the Netherlands, the privatization of the postal service stands as a great success story, almost unique among countries around the world. Perhaps on its way toward the same goal, the postal service of Argentina still faces many new challenges in its own transformation from a state-run enterprise to a well-managed competitive and efficient organization.

The two posts have progressed through the corporatization and divestiture phases at different rates and with different models. PTT Post B.V. in the Netherlands is an extremely progressive postal service which has developed through corporatization and divestiture, and has implemented rigorous commercialization initiatives. Argentina's Encotesa has moved rapidly towards divestiture and will rely on the new concession holders and competitors to drive commercialization initiatives through. Divestiture, as we have seen, is a dynamic process that can take on a variety of different forms. To understand this better, we will examine in more detail what has occurred both in Argentina and in the Netherlands.

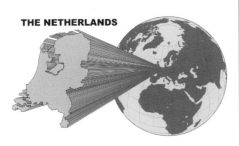

**THE NETHERLANDS**

|  | Netherlands (1995) |
|---|---|
| 1995 GDP (US $ Billions) | 316 |
| 1994 Population (millions) | 15.4 |
| Owner | Government & private |
| 1995 stamp cost (US$) | 43 cents |
| Employees | 36,000 |
| Revenue (US $ billions) | 3.4 |

## A Transformational Triumph

Before he made it his profession, Ad Scheepbouwer's first personal impression of the postal business was that it denied the reality of change. "Postal companies are always on the defensive," said Scheepbouwer, president of PTT Post. "It's nearly always a [case of] denial of any real change taking place."

In 1988, when Scheepbouwer started with the postal service in the Netherlands, the Dutch post was — superficially — succeeding. Costs appeared under control, prices were satisfactory to customers, and employee wages were higher on average than in the private sector. Profitability wasn't an organizational goal; service was. At the time, PTT Post was a national organization comprised primarily of Dutch providers. These providers of postal items delivered principally to Dutch addresses within a monopoly market for the conveyance of letters weighing up to 500 grams. PTT Post discouraged the conveyance of parcels. Politics greatly influenced rate setting. Sales at that time were NLG 3,600 million, with an operating loss of NLG 50 million. Approximately 47,000 employees at PTT Post delivered 5.3 billion items.

Ten years later, and little more than half a decade since the privatization of PTT Post, sales had risen to NLG 6,000 million, with a net profit of NLG 443 million. Yet the number of items delivered had only increased to 6.1 billion, while the total number of employees had actually fallen, to about 36,000. How had this transformation happened?

In part, by changing the ownership structure. Today's PTT Post is a subsidiary of Koninklijke PTT Nederland NV(KPN), a holding company for post and telecommunications that on the first day of 1989 became a corporation that the government wholly owned. Five years later, the government lowered its ownership to about 70 percent after an initial public offering. Then, in October of 1995, the percentage of government ownership dipped below 50 percent after a second stock offering. This reduced the state's interest in KPN to about 45 percent. Today, KPN's shares are quoted on the New York, London and Frankfurt Stock Exchanges.

The revolution at PTT Post actually took place on three fronts — in the market, in the overall structure of the company, and in its internal organization.

"Now we are a service to the public at large," said Scheepbouwer. "But there's no real reason why we can't make money at the same time...We were corporatized on the first of January in 1989. That gave us less political constraints, a company legal base, and more commercial freedom. If you looked at the company then, profit orientation was not a big factor in the minds of people. If you look at specific segments, we had a very massive organization with no profit accountability in any of the smaller areas. Now we have business units that are dedicated to their own market.

"We've had cost control, and that has been very effective and played a large role in our results. The drive to give people the impetus to think about their clients and about the market as the market and not just a public service."

In 1989, with corporatization, the customer became the main focus of the company's business. The company segmented its market into business-to-business and business-to-consumer categories. Foreign companies competed with PTT Posts, especially in courier services. The company gave new, increased attention to parcel services and it separated counter services.

Today, PTT Post serves its segmented markets with seven separate business units, in addition to a joint venture of PTT Post and Postbank called Postkantoren, which provides counter services. With more commercial freedom, PTT Post must not hike its rates in excess of increases in the country's national wage index.

Additionally, PTT Post's rate setting has been subject to complaints by competitors of unfair pricing. To answer these complaints, the Dutch government has been considering a number of equalizing measures. These include loss of the VAT exemptions the business can give to mail order companies and the creation of bulk-mail discounting.

Internally, dedicated interests in markets by each separate business unit have replaced a central organizational interest. In 1985 the main central interest was in managing labor and materials costs. Now, work councils look after employee interests in a context that is cooperative with the interests of the whole company. The implementation of new technologies is ongoing. Presently, a project is underway that will result in a 98 percent automated sorting operation. The company has already successfully put in place tracking and tracing systems for courier and parcel services.

"From 1989 to 1994, when the first third of the company was sold, I think we achieved well," said Ad Scheepbouwer. Now boasting more than a hundred thousand shareholders, the company is owned partly by its employees because 31,000 stockholders are employees.

One of the great advantages of being privatized is the boldness with which PTT Post can explore new avenues for revenue making. It has started a niche mail-order company called Telekado. Print and mail centers, started two years ago, offer hybrid services primarily for invoices. The post is even exploring the sale of prescription drugs by direct mail. PTT Post also runs a venture with the Dutch airline KLM.

"I think if you look back on how [we] lived up to our expectations," concludes Scheepbouwer, "it's control of [your] company, knowing what you're doing. [And] you have to have some creativity that your big growth areas can be fueled and then you have to hope that these live up to the expectations of the investors."

Nevertheless, because competition is increasing both in the Netherlands and abroad, profit margins are getting smaller. Moreover, competitive threats to the monopoly increased further when Algemene Postdienst Nederlands (APN) said it was going to begin to deliver unaddressed mailings and other kinds of "non-letters" in the country. APN, an alternative delivery firm, hopes to underprice PTT Post's rates with a goal of delivering a million mail items each week in this highly competitive market. In response, PTT Post hopes to increase the number of postal outlets that it franchises while realizing savings of employee costs of the equivalent of approximately 9,000 FTEs over a five-year period ending in 1999.

As *Postal Performance* was being researched, Ad Scheepbouwer told us that, looking to the future, PTT's next step would be the distribution of postal items abroad. In the fall of 1996, KPN made a successful bid for the global courier group TNT. The enlarged KPN group will offer services in 200 countries with its own operations in 47 countries, and will carry more than two million items of freight each week. It will be the largest time-sensitive courier and postal group in Europe.

The transaction will combine TNT's domestic time-sensitive distribution and logistics businesses in Italy, Germany, France and the UK, as well as in the Americas, Australia and Asia; with PTT's domestic businesses within the Netherlands, Germany, Belgium, Austria and Denmark, as well as its international mail services; and with the international time-sensitive services in GD Express Worldwide (GDEW). This deal will obviously have far-reaching implications within the industry.

The main strength of the combined group will be within Europe, where it will become a major player across several segments: in a number of domestic markets (the United Kingdom, Germany, Italy and the Netherlands); within the international remail business (Mailfast); in the intra-European parcel and freight business GD Express Worldwide; and in the logistics business.

A significant area of weakness for the new group will be North America, the home of two significant integrators, Federal Express and United Parcel Service. Both companies already have strong brand awareness and customer loyalty. Their significant domestic networks support intercontinental traffic flows, which any other player is going to find difficult to compete against. The domestic operations of these integrators have supported expansion in their international operations.

Asia, on the other hand, represents the true battleground for the integrators, each of which is struggling to assert itself in the region. DHL, Federal Express and TNT have established (or soon will) an intra-Asian air network. For TNT, this is proving a costly investment, with capacity issues and revenue quality challenging local management. Nevertheless, the proposed deal strongly positions PTT Post in the international market — a position which could only have been taken by a privatized company.

PTT Post's ability to remain profitable rests on its privatization, concluded Ad Scheepbouwer. But he cautioned other posts contemplating the Dutch example. "One of the things that we learned from our privatization process is: first thing first," Scheepbouwer said. In other words, to achieve transformational success, you must first build what Scheepbouwer calls a "lean and mean" organization.

In the Netherlands, therefore, PTT Post is forced to operate as a commercial concern to meet its shareholder's demands. And it continues to operate under some monopoly protection against competition.

In Argentina, on the other hand, the government has actively encouraged competition to force the public postal service to improve effectiveness and also to support the national business infrastructure.

| | Argentina (1995) |
|---|---|
| 1995 GDP (US $ Billions) | 284 |
| 1994 Population (millions) | 34.2 |
| Owner | Government |
| 1995 stamp cost (US$) | 75 cents |
| Employees | 20,037 |
| Revenue (US $ billions) | 0.45 |

**ARGENTINA**

## A Diversity of Ownership

In 1989, when Carlos Menem became its leader, Argentina was in the midst of a severe financial crisis. The Argentinean Congress took action, passing a new law that among other measures dramatically changed the way the country's post office did business. The new law defined procedures for Congress to declare any business run by the state "privatizable" in part or whole. The law further gave the executive branch of government the power to eliminate monopoly clauses and other discriminatory privileges that might inhibit initiatives leading to privatization.

Three years later, in 1992, a decree based on the 1989 law transformed Argentina's National Posts and Telegraphs Enterprise — known as Encotel — into a corporation with a limited privatized structure. The name of the new corporation was Empressa Nacional de Correos y Telegrafos SA, or Encotesa. The internal administration of this new company was very similar to that of a private limited corporation. The liberalization of the postal service also led to the creation of a new regulatory body called Comission National de Correos y

Telegrafos (National Posts and Telegraphs Commission), or CNCT, which remains responsible for ensuring that free competition does not violate specific rights of postal customers.

The decree also made provision in due course for the adoption of a mixed privatization system for the new limited company, with shares held jointly by the state (51 percent), corporation employees (14 percent), and public postal operators on the open international market (35 percent). The existing partial deregulation of Argentina's postal market led in 1993 to another decree that abolished the state's postal monopoly. This 1993 decree opened up the local and international mail market to competition. It also created a national register of postal service providers in Argentina, and it specifically required that the public postal administration provide basic universal service without any reserved services.

None of this progress came without a price, however. Political scandal accompanied many of the achievements of the postal service in Argentina, requiring strong action by Domingo Cavallo, the country's economy minister.

Encotesa's creation and the subsequent appointment of a new senior management team drawn largely from the private sector has halted the decline in the company's fortunes, restored financial stability, and transformed not only the operation but the image of postal services in Argentina. *Correo Argentino* as a brand name is now a market leader.

The anticipated change in the running of Argentina's post will represent a radical departure from the inefficiencies of the past. Almost 30 years ago, the former National Corporation of Posts and Telegraphs (Encotel) assumed responsibility for the country's postal office operations. For nearly 20 years, Encotel operated with the primary obligation of providing universal postal service, with a provision for a few small companies, called permissionarios, to compete with Encotel for certain specified services. These permissionarios paid a royalty to Encotel.

Despite the royalty, which was equivalent to the price of an ordinary letter, Encotel's revenues and volume declined sharply, first in bulk mail and then in first class. By 1993, Encotel's volume had dropped by 70 percent. As a result, Encotel was increasingly restricted to less profitable geographic areas and products. Eventually, the permissionarios were able to increase their premium service prices. By then, a national postal system that had first been established a century before, in 1876, was in dire need of the reforms that the decree of 1993 ushered in — partly because there was a very significant black market in operation as well.

The black market grew so that illegal operators could avoid paying royalties. Legally, if a company wanted to provide postal services, it had to register with the regulator and then pay for every item of mail it carried. Customers did not know whether they were dealing with a licensed or unlicensed operator. They simply bought mail service from a company.

After the decree, Encotel was recapitalized and refounded as Encotesa, with the same operating assets but an increase in paid-up capital. The state retained Encotel's residual liabilities, while a new management team took control. To maximize the benefits of competition, the newly deregulated postal service reduced prices by removing the royalty paid by the permissionarios, encouraging development of new products and services, particularly in the sector of advertising mail, and increasing the quality of basic mail services. Encotesa's market share began to rise as market prices began to fall.

By the end of 1995 the CNCT had issued private postal licenses to nearly 300 companies to operate postal services in the country. Under law, these companies guarantee the continuity, regularity, and scope of those services. As a consequence, Argentina has seen the growth of priority services, including tracking and tracing previously unavailable, and an innovative approach to postal savings accounts. Direct mail is still relatively undeveloped and fragmented, but Encotesa is moving forward aggressively with plans to develop new market databases and to assist in direct marketing. Encotesa has also set service standards for basic mail service.

Prior to the deregulation of the Argentinean postal market, the average price for the delivery of public service bills was $1.75, VAT included, according to Jose Guillermo Capdevila, president of CNCT. That figure has fallen 65 percent to $.60. The total volume of postal items has risen 40 percent, from 449 million per year to 645 million annually. However, revenue for postal services has also increased, though not by as much—from $775 million annually to $968 million (including VAT). The average effectiveness of the postal service within the federal capital has risen impressively from 72 percent to 98 percent in on-time deliveries.

Internal transformation of Encotesa is responsible for many of these results. Encotesa has developed a distinctive yellow and blue logo that is visible on its products, and it has released many new philatelic issues under the slogan, "La Cultura de una Nacion." Encotesa has also set up an account program for its large customer and implemented greatly improved customer service. Interestingly, employment levels have fallen substantially, from over 26,000 in 1993 to under 20,000 just two years later. Yet there have been no labor strikes, and productivity has risen.

Within metropolitan Buenos Aires, Encotesa has completely reorganized its postal operations. The remodeling of national operations and transport networks has led to a better structure and more controllable networks. Remodeling of the distribution network has followed. Customer service surveys demonstrate the success of these strategies: Encotesa now ranks second in the level of national satisfaction with postal operators. In fact, Encotesa's satisfaction level has jumped 50 points in just two years, according to its own research surveys.

"Clearly, the world postal system is presently undergoing a transformation and none of those involved in this sector, particularly operators, governments and the private sector, can go forward alone," says CNCT's President Capdevila.

Today the Argentine government is moving toward a form of full privatization through the likely sale to a strategic buyer of a concession to operate Encotesa's services. Since 1989, the vast majority of other state-owned businesses in Argentina have already been privatized. The country hopes that the complete privatization of Encotesa will enhance its service delivery with higher quality standards at the same time that it reduces tariffs, frees Encotesa to compete for new business, and fosters growth in the range, quality, and availability of services.

**Different Paths to Progress**

The customers of both the Dutch and Argentine postal services are receiving a higher quality competitive service as a result of decisions to divest. However, as we have seen, the results have been achieved by different means.

Divestiture itself will take different forms. PTT Post had undergone significant transformation prior to its sale on the public stock exchange. Consequently, it was an attractive business to the so-called uninvolved shareholders, who play no role in day to day management.

Conversely, Encotesa in Argentina must continue to change to survive in the competitive, non-monopoly, post-divestiture market. It needs an operator who can visualize the potential of the business and contribute to the achievement of that vision—a vision of postal performance that, in one form or another, most posts around the world will address in the future.

# Chapter

# 9

## SMOOTHING THE CHANGE— THE CORPORATE TRANSFORMATION FRAMEWORK

*'It is possible that the trauma of change is now a necessity for most organizations....as firms attempt to adjust to shifting market demands, grapple with aggressive new and desperate old competitors, exploit changing technology, and respond to a plethora of emerging customer standards — what was hitherto considered excellence is now the norm, and the goal is the satisfaction of unanticipated customer requirements.'*
— Paul Taffinder in *The New Leaders*

For the complacent postal executive — or regulator, or government official — mere awareness of the drivers of change within the postal environment may not be enough to commence the transformation process necessary to make a post competitive, responsive and businesslike. Those executives who truly want dramatic improvement in the performance of their organizations and have the vision and endurance to see it through, will commence this transformation process. For many that process may well start with a series of self-addressed questions:

*What do I want the world of posts to be?*

*Have I the power to change?*

*Where do I go next?*

*What do I say to my minister?*

*What do I say to my staff?*

*What do I say to my customers?*

Answering these questions is easy. Answering them with sufficient insight to make a real difference is not. The fact is that anyone can kick off a huge change program, but as postal services struggle to adapt to continuous change and shape that adaptation as a competitive advantage, they must formulate responses that enable them to make major, corporate-wide, integrated changes that are more far reaching than single solutions to individual problems. And that is a difficult proposition.

Posts have responded to the challenges faced by the industry by adopting many of the new management theories and approaches ranging from total quality management to business process reengineering — with widely varying degrees of success. Large numbers of projects have been initiated with piecemeal improvements failing to achieve a real breakthrough. Clearly, what is needed is an integrated strategic management and operational improvement approach to achieving the new standards of performance that will be required as we approach the next century.

This is a journey on which a post — or any other organization — travels in partnership with its leaders, its workforce and its advisors. In this chapter, we'll try to provide a glimpse of the path this transformation journey can and should follow. We'll first describe Coopers & Lybrand's Corporate Transformation Framework and then look at an organization — in this case, a large European insurance company — that's already begun this process and whose experience can be illustrative for a post embarking on a transformation initiative.

**Transformation Is Unique to Each Organization**

Transformation is highly contextual, with each transformation being unique to the organization concerned — each organization faces different challenges with a singular set of resources. Generally, however, we take it to mean a process where the organization redefines its strategy and sustains a program of dramatic change. Transformational change usually is characterized by strong visionary leadership, an obsession with customer focus, a commitment to breakthrough and then continuous process improvement, and the alignment of both people and processes behind organizational goals and objectives.

The following factors are likely to be present if an organization is ready for transformation:
- The external threat or opportunity is sufficiently *fundamental* and *compelling* to require *significant* change to most and possibly all of the orga-

nization's existing strategy, objectives, products, business methods, processes, structures, cost structures, systems, competencies and culture.

- The change required is wider than could be achieved through any single approach (such as downsizing or systems strategy) or even simple combinations. Transformation involves coordinating and integrating *multiple approaches* to deliver the required changes.

As Paul Taffinder has noted in *The New Leaders*, "Let's take all of these themes together - global change, competitive pressures, restructuring and reengineering, total organizational renewal, industry and executive reinvention. What follows from this? Well, there is a need for an approach which does three things:....helps [business leaders] to understand the 'mess' with which they are confronted every day: the current position of their organization in respect of its markets, core competencies, competitors and culture; gets leaders to break out of the box and redraw their organization's future...[and] ensures that all the useful tactics of change (BPR, restructuring, and culture change) can be integrated, made to produce more than simple incremental change."

Some aspects of organizational transformation are common to all industries, postal included. First, transformation *commences at the strategic level*. While not all transformations will require a fundamental change of strategic goals or specific strategies, there is at least a need to challenge, reexamine and update any existing strategy within the context of the external environment and other drivers of change. Some term this "building the burning platform" — that is, making things so uncomfortable that there is no alternative but to change. Whatever the characterization, the organization has to be shown what will happen if the enterprise tries to maintain the status quo, and that also there is an attractive outcome to be realized. Second, it is highly likely that the transformation approach will be *unique* to the organization in question. In other words there is not a "one size fits all" blueprint for transformation. Third, the transformation is likely to require the implementation of new and perhaps radically different ideas and concepts for doing business. Fourth, the transformation will typically be *led by a strong central individual such as the CEO*, able to articulate a vision to drive the transformation and motivate others to implement and enact it.

Finally, transformation is about people — managers, employees, suppliers and customers — and their capacity to accommodate new ways of behaving and of getting work done. High levels of customer satisfaction, innovation and technology are not achieved unless the leaders align all employees to their vision. Employees must understand the compelling need for change, and they must see that their innovative ideas for improvement are readily accepted. Success only derives from managing the change process: setting realistic expectations for an organization's ability to change, introducing change at a pace that the organization can assimilate, and insuring that change leaders have a strong internal base of support.

### The Proper Approach: A Framework, Not A Single Methodology

Because of the scale of change required to achieve each transformation in culture, structure and performance, and because each organization's transformation requirements are unique, a single methodology will never suffice. Rather, the requirement is to mix and tailor relevant approaches to address each of the areas required for the transformation in a way that enables the enterprise to carry on its business while maintaining the change program.

We recommend an approach that provides a *structured framework* with separate, fully tailorable elements which assist organizations to accomplish six goals. First, to assess challenges (threats or opportunities), and against these, their capability to respond. Second, to respond creatively, creating a new purpose and exciting vision of the future of the organization. Third, to challenge, reexamine and, where necessary, revise the organization's strategy. Fourth, to identify and prioritize the program of changes which will result in the transformation sought. Fifth, to specify, blue-print and implement those changes. And, finally, to measure their progress and results.

The separate elements require sophisticated methodologies in their own right. Our firm, Coopers & Lybrand, has considerable experience in each. Our methodologies have been constructed in a highly modular yet interlinked way, and are underpinned by common techniques and tools. Rather than a 'mass produced' service which forces an organization's requirements to fit a rigid framework, transformation programs are customized and configured to meet the particular requirements of each business.

In the end, a business transformation succeeds or fails on the efforts of the organization itself. No amount of advice, no degree of counsel, no program of training will be sufficient if the business itself has not embraced the need for transformation, and undertaken the effort and understanding needed to accomplish that process.

## The Stages of Transformation

The overall framework for transformation, which we introduced in Chapter Two, uses the wheel as its

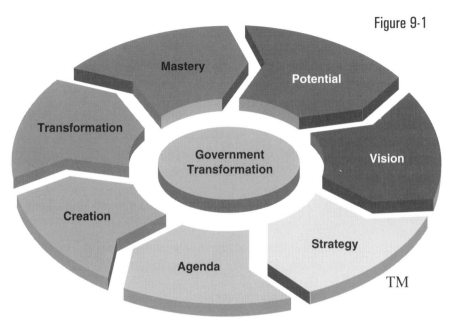

Figure 9-1

structural model. In fact, it's a cycle of broad stages (see Figure 9-1).

Transformation begins by an organization addressing its *potential*. This phase involves intensive assessment. The Chief Executive Officer, the Executive Leadership Team, and the Board form a view of the current and future factors in their environment which are likely to influence the business as well as the range of possible opportunities that may exist and that the organization might choose to exploit; its capability to innovate and respond; and the resulting potential for achieving a transformation.

The CEO, the Executive Leadership Team, and the Board then develop a *vision*, defining the future they want for the business, in terms of its purpose, value proposition and strategic architecture. The vision should be comprehensive in scope and detailed in its description. The vision must act as a focal point for the change effort: to achieve this it must be aspirational yet able to engage the interest of all the stakeholders of the business.

If an enterprise's vision specifies the 'what', the next phase —- *strategy* — defines the 'how' of the transformation. This phase concentrates on the development of viable business strategies, leading to a decision on the best strategy — one that portends the greatest expected value. What are the broad capabilities the organization will require to achieve its vision? What are the main change components of the transformation and the critical success factors for achieving it? The answers flow from the strategy development.

Next comes the assembly of an *agenda*. The organization now configures the coordinated, feasible program of business changes which will make up the transformation. *Creation* — blue-printing, testing and planning the changes which will create the new business — follows. This includes products, processes, structures, systems, costs and culture - as well as reshaping the corporate portfolio where this is required.

In the *transformation* stage, the new business 'becomes real', implementing the radical changes required to deliver the transformation. Implementation is where "the rubber meets the road" — the phase in which change actually happens. Throughout this phase, it is essential for the organization to focus "like a laser beam" on the new vision, customers, and aligning people and processes with the new organizational goals and objectives. This alignment is the goal of effective change management in a transformational effort.

Success leads to *mastery*, the final phase. Here, the organization continues the transformation, learning to exploit the possibilities of, and grow within, the new paradigm. This is the phase in which continuous improvement and continuous learning become an integral part of the culture and processes. Just as change does not stop, so the business cannot stand still once the transformation has been initially implemented.

**The Case of Capitol Insurance**

To see how the transformation approach applies to an organization, consider the case of Capitol Insurance (not its real name). Capitol is a wholly-owned sub-sidiary of a European-headquartered corporation, has been in business for more than a century, and stands in the top quartile of all insurers operating in its national marketplace. With more than $5 billion in funds under management, Capitol today posts an annual net of close to a half billion in revenues, and the value of its longterm business is twice that. Nevertheless, at the start of this decade, Capitol — in the words of one of its senior managers — "was at the edge of a precipice" (see Figure 9-2).

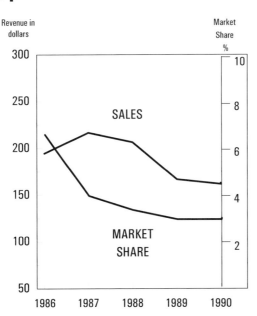

**Capitol Insurance Performance**

Figure 9-2

Problems created by a recession in its home country were exacerbated by growing competition, by a wave of scandal and fraud throughout the industry, and by increasingly tough regulation designed to protect consumers. The internal and external threats to performance included a rigid and costly operating framework devised by regulators, competition from banks, and shrinkage within Capitol's traditional markets, principally those related to mortgages. Falling revenues driven by declining market share and fewer sales were coupled with an increasing level of mistrust among staff and a growing reputation among customers for, as one put it, "lousy service". As the decade began, Capitol's leadership concluded that a transformation program was critical.

## Mobilization

Committing to an eight-year effort, Capitol decided the program was, above all, necessary for the organization's survival. Using the Corporate Transformation Wheel model, Capitol began by quickly restructuring itself in the first nine months — reducing staff by one-third, then introducing business process redesign, total quality and staff involvement programs. Those initiatives linked to six phases on the model: potential, vision, strategy, agenda, creation and transformation. The transformation program, Capitol's senior managers understood, would have to both initially address the survival of the business and ensure longterm success. Companywide initiatives would channel staff energy and commitment in the same direction. A culture supporting self-development would be spawned, inspired by values and behavior modeled by Capitol's leadership.

## Potential

While the organization was addressing the need for 'financial headroom' through the initial staff reductions, Capitol immediately began a strategic review to address the *potential* for transformational success, looking at both the external environment and internal capability. The review established that there were several severe organizational weaknesses: excessive spending levels, poor internal organizational and financial controls, inadequate management information, overreliance on residential sales, outdated IT systems and slow product development. Management concluded that, even in a costcutting environment, new investment in information technology was required. And Capitol also realized that cost reductions had to be carefully planned, in order to minimize their impact on customer service.

## Vision

At the time, Capitol's only operating *vision* was to survive. That, all agreed, was inadequate to successfully drive the company's longterm transformation. Over three years, a new vision evolved: to "promote Capitol Insurance as a dynamic and customer-focused business"; to "delight the customer with its service"; to "offer products which were value for money"; and to "achieve excellent profits for shareholders." The vision statement continues to be revised as the transformation program moves forward. A staff charter and a new set of values to guide behavior is being developed through employee efforts and an internal communications program. "Leading a change program like this is a bit like being the pilot of a jet," noted a Capitol manager, "When you've committed to take off, you have no choice but to keep going."

Noteworthy here was the fact that the vision statement followed the downsizing. As Paul Taffinder says, "There is a logical sequence to any program of big change. In developing our Corporate Transformation framework, it was obvious to us that resolving the immediate crisis was crucial to the success of any transformation effort. When your backs are up against the wall, you need to sort that problem first before launching into anything else." The desire to survive is as powerful a motivator for change as a clear and detailed longterm vision. Involvement of the employees in developing the vision, at an appropriate point, will begin to model stated values about teamwork and empowerment. But any vision statement needs revisiting time and time again — particularly when a transformation is pushing rapid and dramatic cultural change.

## Strategy

Following the strategic review, the first phase of Capitol's *strategy* began. One major element was — as we've indicated — costcutting (see Figure 9-3). But the business improvement program also included restructuring and an additional review of administration processes. Staff numbers were systematically reduced by a third over six months. Seventy percent of those found new employment. There was no union or staff opposition. In addition, plans were put in place for a $70 million investment in information technology, with full implementation due by the eighth year of the transformation. A Total Quality initiative quickly followed, with six critical business processes earmarked for redesign. A second strategic phase, which still continues, consists of customer-focused cultural change, staff involvement and continuous improvement projects. In Capitol's

## Capitol Insurance Cost Savings

Figure 9-3

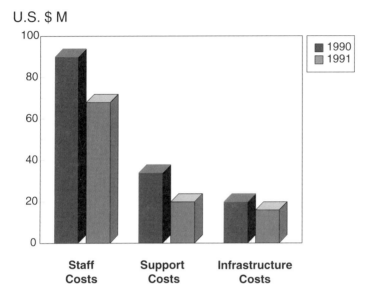

Client Services Division alone, 174 continuous improvement teams operate.

In the strategy phase, Capitol first addressed its financial crisis. When survival was assured, the firm could progress to a more sophisticated strategy. In the CEO's words, "We needed enough headroom, in terms of funds, credibility and time, to be able to tackle the really big challenges." Nevertheless, Capitol was careful to plan its costcutting, rather than execute an across-the-board approach. Its clear strategic focus gave Capitol a "personality"; one that could be communicated to its clients through experience, rather than advertising.

### Agenda

Capitol next began setting a forward-looking, long-term change *agenda*. The transformation agenda, it is important to remember, is concerned with identifying, sequencing and assembling the coordinated program of business changes, so that the vision of the transformed organization can be realized. Supporting this agenda was an ever-increasing emphasis on employee involvement, which became a business objective in itself. "In the end," recalled one Capitol executive, "we had to tackle many more things than we had first envisaged." The examination of end-to-end critical business processes was identified as the vehicle for change — in order to increase both staff and customer satisfaction by eliminating the functional focus. These processes and supporting performance indicators then became a catalyst for a new way of looking at issues that resulted in significant improvements in quality.

In more recent stages of the transformation, management style and behavior have been pushed to the top of the agenda. The success of the Quality Team set the scene for an ongoing, all-embracing, participative approach to improving performance. Now a detailed project plan has been produced for the implementation of the customer-focused program incorporating cultural change and continuous improvement. The plan has a cascading approach to target and milestone-setting and monitoring. The process has set up very tight and systematic time scales for the achievement of each task within the wider project framework. It is overseen by director-level project sponsors. A key element of the Capitol agenda has been the systematic investment in a multi-skilled work force. Each employee understands the configuration of their process and how their skills contribute to the overall objective or task. With ambitious goals and milestones, people have been motivated to leave their "comfort zones". But those milestones had to be carefully programmed and monitored.

## Creation

"Every single employee was aware," said one Capitol manager, "of the targets and time scales that were required." That awareness reflected the activities of the *creation* phase on the Corporate Transformation Wheel, where Capitol's leadership recognized that the company couldn't survive without effective information systems. At the same time, it was accepted that the payback from implementing a nearly $100 million system would take a significant time to be realized. Accordingly, a new structure put in place had to anticipate systems deliverables that were at least two years away.

With Capitol's six critical business processes identified, teams were established to map the processes from end to end. Following the mapping four years ago, teams representing the critical processes were set up. All teams, including small corporate specialist teams created to determine policy and strategy for the core business disciplines, worked under a companywide steering committee. That steering group, in turn, drafted a range of performance indicators to enhance the effective management of the six processes. The steering group also defined the type of employee required to make the new processes and culture succeed: "thought workers" and "service professionals", rather than traditional clerical staff. Strategies were put in place to recruit, train and retain highly-skilled administrative staff who, in turn, adopted a mature approach to flexible ways of working. "It was fantastic that, because we'd thought through the coordinated program of changes during the 'agenda' phase, we were able to change the organization first," said a steering committee member, "and then the systems. In the past the reverse has always applied."

Key to the success of the creation phase was the understanding that transformation requires highly-skilled project management. The establishment and monitoring of challenging objectives, with specific responsibilities and time frames, must be all-pervasive and clearly communicated. At the same time, company-wide initiatives provide coherence and a sense of team-work. They may also capitalize on the opportunities presented by tailoring projects to a local level and addressing specific issues. Finally, developing the concept of the internal customer helped break down barriers between departments, processes and functions.

**Transformation**

At present, Capitol Insurance is immersed in its *transformation* phase — making the radical changes required to deliver the vision. *Mastery* lies a year or two yet down the road, although building the foundation for continuous improvement and continuous learning are integral concepts in the various aspects of the transformation phase. The results of positively managing change are already evident (see Figure 9-4). Three years after the transformation program began, Capitol posted a 32 percent increase in annual profits, and a 35 percent reduction in annual expenses. Customer satisfaction improved. Staff surveys showed employee morale on the rise.

The important elements of the transformation phase have included organization-wide staff involvement; a commitment to new behaviors, and cultural change; a realistic approach to systems implementation; and the introduction of service-level agreements between departments. For Capitol, the effort to involve all employees in the change began after the initial staff reductions took place. Managers went through a process

## Capitol Insurance Performance Figure 9-4

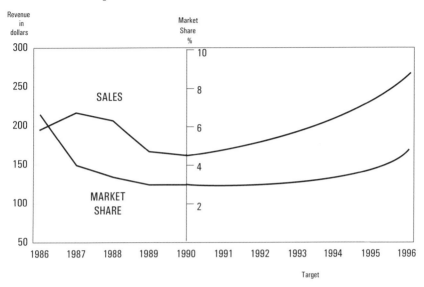

of collectively and individually examining both their strengths and weaknesses, and the role of the teams to which they'd been assigned. They introduced a 360-degree feedback system. Massive efforts went towards communications — as they had during each other phase, particularly concerning the leadership of change. "I wanted to communicate personally," says the CEO, "with as many staff as possible, especially when we were going through the tough times, when one in three of our colleagues was losing his or her job. The communication process at times involved me in three or four roadshow events a day for weeks....But it was vital to keep people focused on the future and give them an opportunity to ask me questions that were worrying them."

Staff at every level were encouraged to motivate and educate themselves. The continuous improvement teams received and reacted to employee suggestions. And the concept of "manager as coach" was introduced to help develop a learning culture within the firm. "The end of our systems implementation, two years ahead, feels like the great unknown," concluded a member of Capitol's leadership. "Yet that will only be the start. Frankly, it's been tremendously challenging, but also very exciting."

## The Postal Lesson

For the global postal industry, buffeted by competition, by changing markets, by substitute technologies, the lessons of companies and organizations like Capitol can be valuable in meeting these challenges and establishing a new advantage. And, as we have stated several times, transformational change is becoming an absolute necessity for posts throughout the world. In effective transformations, existing thinking is challenged and staff stimulated to identify new ways of doing business. Postal leaders have already begun to take this approach in many countries. The key is not to simply 'rearrange the deck chairs' but achieve genuine and lasting transformation.

In the next chapter, we'll try to delineate where we see the most challenging situations in the global postal industry emerging in the years ahead. We term these "The Big Questions." The answers we offer, we hope, begin to mark the path this journey to the future will take.

# Chapter

# 10

## FUTURE POST

*In 1995, the World Bank — to commemorate its 50th year —
conducted a debate to develop what became a vision statement.
We realized we could talk about a range of issues, and act in a
range of areas, that previously were out of bounds.*
— Jan Piercy,
United States Executive Director of The World Bank

What was remarkable, the World Bank's Kumar Ranganathan realized as he surveyed the Berne, Switzerland auditorium where the Universal Postal Union's April 1996 conference on postal development and reform was being held, was not simply his listeners' attentiveness. It was the size of the audience. Representatives of the governments and postal administrations of more than 100 countries were in attendance.

The announcement that the World Bank, with its nearly $170 billion in assets, was prepared to invest in postal reform, was a global attention-getter.

"There is a need for reform in the postal sector," said Ranganathan, the bank executive who had led an in-depth study of postal reform in Australia, Canada, Chile, Singapore, Sweden, the United Kingdom and 29 other countries. "This need is particularly evident and urgent in low-income and middle-income countries."

As Ranganathan began to enumerate the areas most ripe for reform, his audience leaned forward. Financial performance, the executive said, was problematic in less wealthy nations — 10 to 20 times worse than high-income countries. Commercialization, and to a lesser extent corporatization, had had success in reforming enterprises where it had been tried. Regulatory reform — the liberalization of the marketplace — had had success, too, though on a more limited basis. Linking the two, suggested Ranganathan, offered the most opportunity.

The best route to profitable reform, argued Ranganathan, was one that combined modernization through investment, new service offerings and strategic alliances. All posts, said Ranganathan, had to recognize that they were in the communications business. Adapting to the changing technologies affecting communications was key to any future success, the World Bank representative emphasized.

"Unless the postal service integrates communications technology into its service provision," warned Ranganathan, "the economics and the changing market preferences may prevent the post from providing a truly universal service."

That was the bad news. The good was that the World Bank's lending program, for the first time, would be directed towards the global postal sector. Outside investors would be taking careful note. The audience got the message: let the competition for funding begin.

## Where Change Will Occur

As Kumar Ranganathan suggested, there are a number of influences pushing the world's postal sector towards 21st century change. Liberalized telecom markets cross boundaries. Microchip power is increasing, and prices are dropping. More people and businesses use personal computers, and networks, for communications and commerce. Behaviors are being transformed.

Later in this chapter, we'll specify where competition will emerge, what new customer demands may encompass, how new supplier relationships may be structured, and what monopoly protection and universal service mandate erosion is likely. We'll also examine how taxation, ownership, relations with labor, and the universal tariff may be transformed. But first we'll look at the impacts of industry trends on the infrastructure of postal services.

The factors creating the greatest impact on postal services are the *economy, technology, financial services,* (which impacts both the letter mail volume and the retail counters business of postal services), the *distribution industries* (courier companies and freight forwarders, which influence the parcels distribution activities of postal services), the *advertising industry* (where postal direct mail is one medium amongst many); and the *communications market* (where fundamental changes come through the convergence of telecommunications, information technology, and consumer electronics). All are combining to escalate the volume of communication transactions in the market. And although post is constantly losing market share, it still has the capacity to grow absolute volumes because the market is growing so rapidly. Communication seems to be breeding communication.

## Recognized Differences

Our readers know — and the authors recognize — there are differences in postal operations, markets, statutory authorities, regulatory environments and other factors differentiating postal administrations. Obviously, one view does not fit all. We believe our observations and conclusions generally apply, though the unique differences by country and region are too numerous to address on a case-by-case basis.

## Where Is the Competitive Advantage?

*Operations*
The mail system has changed. It is no longer piece-by-piece "pigeonholed". Mail is now largely computer-and-high-speed-printer-generated, originating from extensive databases and inserted into mail distribution at different points near to the delivery office. It is processed in postal distribution operations using manufacturing flow techniques to handle staggering volumes at high speed and delivered daily to every business and household address.

That developed countries' postal systems depend on technology to a great extent is not well understood by

the public. Many postal systems use cutting-edge technology in areas such as optical character recognition,
database management, robotics and artificial intelligence to manage their basic business. They also use
sophisticated communications and information-process-
ing techniques to handle their customer relationships
and to provide value-added customer services. To the
extent these technologies require great effort and
resources to replicate, they provide formidable barriers
to entry for potential competitors.

In addition, large customers have invested great
amounts of capital and expertise to develop within their
firms the operating systems that are the originators of
the mail pieces the postal systems deliver. In the most
advanced economies, the linking of the customers' systems with those of the postal services is starting to provide an integrated, end-to-end system that will manage
and track customer communications in a real-time
mode. While such systems already exist for packages,
the extension of the technology to letters and packets
will be a quantum leap in terms of the resources needed
to provide the service. Again, this will raise barriers to
entry. For example, in the United States, the Postal
Service is introducing for major customers a service
called "Fast Forward", which provides address correc-
tions that allow mailers to learn about address changes
to their customer lists before the mail piece is entered
into the mail stream. The corrected piece thus avoids
being sent to the old address first and then forwarded,
saving effort and time for the end-to-end system. As
custodians of the national address database, posts are
uniquely equipped to play a dominant role as systems
and techniques become more and more sophisticated.

There will be, of course, differing approaches to
how technology is used by the posts and how they share
responsibility for the end-to-end system with their cus-

tomers. Some posts will seek to integrate backwards, providing as much value-added services as they can, while others will try to be partners with various players in the whole supply chain, seeking to dominate their part of the chain while allowing others to provide value-added services as well. The bottom line is that the seemingly simple business of mailing a letter — the oldest of the communication channels — is, in reality, every bit as technology-dependent as other channels. Understanding this is critical for success for posts and their customers.

Historically, posts' source of long-term sustainable advantage has been in their ubiquitous delivery network. But as the postal markets liberalize, competitors are moving into markets and setting up more efficient networks feeding into the posts' own. Competitors could — in end-to-end costs — end up below the postal services'.

Is this delivery advantage really sustainable in the long run? We think so, but only by moving aggressively to connect electronically to the source of the mail. To some degree, this is already underway, and is very costly to replicate when combined with delivery. It is a big competitive advantage in a "mature" but economically viable industry. To protect the absolute scale across the whole postal network, postal services need to increase complexity for some classes of mail to make the networks less easy to replicate. They can do that by adding value up the chain before the delivery point. This is why postal services will be capturing much more data from transactions. There are, however, competitive advantages in the high-density delivery of advertising mail, publications and packages, to encourage — through pricing strategies — entry into the postal network closer to the delivery unit.

In some cases, posts' distribution systems will be connected directly into the sending customers' computer systems. Posts will have the choice of capturing physical postal items — letters — or capturing the information electronically and deciding where and in what sequence to print them. That decision will be based upon when the sending customer wants the item delivered, how much they're prepared to pay for the delivery, and what kind of information they want attached to the delivery. The whole environment will become sophisticated, and less easy to replicate. Today, most innovation in the core network can be found in the USA (in the use of robotics and artificial intelligence) and in some of the smaller, highly developed services such as in Denmark and New Zealand.

*Product Portfolio — Communications, Distribution, Pricing*

Postal services today are implementing hybrid services at the edge of their system. The volumes are low; the transactions are specialized. But the hybrid notion may be a red herring. More than 80 percent of letters transactions start in a customer's computer. The vast majority of letters, in other words, are already hybrids. The postal intervention simply happens further down the chain than it needs to. If a postal service was hooked directly into the customer's computer, printing could happen anywhere within the postal system.

Delivery of the finished product would contain options. A customer could be told, "If you want this delivered this afternoon at all destinations, then we are prepared to print locally for you. That will cost extra because we can't achieve the scale economies in the printing environment. If you're happy for it to be delivered tomorrow morning, then you print or we'll print at a couple of main sorting centers, and physically carry it through the network. If you're happy for it to be delivered in a couple of days time, then we'll print it in one center and the transaction will take longer to transport."

Linking operations with product development in response to customer needs is one of the significant features of the future. In the past, operations have been divorced from marketing, requiring customer conformance with operations systems. That must end.

Better segmentation and understanding the real sources of added value perceived by their customers at both ends, sending and receiving, will lead to a more responsive range of products with various levels of attached features. And the quicker, the better. It's the key to long-term sustainable scale.

Finally, we predict that this more complex product and product feature structure will transform the pricing tables. Regulators will start to become more interested in how postal services are executing their pricing. Competitors will challenge price levels. The universal tariff will become much less significant.

*Management*

In the future, postal administrations are going to have to become more strategic, faster, and more comfortable with risk-taking because they — depending upon the economy and impact of technology — will no longer enjoy a reasonably predictable, steady-volume-growth core business. Today's issues will seem simple in comparison to what lies ahead. The operations environment will be much more technology-oriented. Joint ventures and partnerships will emerge. Customers will expect satisfaction of complicated needs.

On financing, postal balance sheets' structure may change to permit raising private loans. This will lead to different forms of financing entering the sector. We're beginning to see it already. Australia Post is able to raise loan capital on the open market. And as more risks are taken and more partnerships entered, the more likely it is that we'll see more complex balance sheets evolving. The clearest example to watch in the short term is KPN and PTT Post in the Netherlands.

## What Type of Post Will Emerge?

Today's global postal industry can be divided into three categories: the U.S. Postal Service; developed posts; and posts in emerging, typically developing-national markets.

The United States Postal Service dwarfs the others in size, volume and revenues, and is unique both in that regard and in its relationship with its government and its ratesetting commission. The USPS is trying hard to go along a commercialization path, but it's hampered in many respects by its political, legal and regulatory environment, and also by significant and unusual lobbying pressures from its competitors, customer groups and unions.

Developed postal services — primarily those in the western world — have been concentrating on and advancing in commercialization, working to improve quality of service, to adopt a profit motivation or a pseudo-profit motivation, and to use private sector practices for their management.

The developed posts have been improving efficiency in their networks. They've been experimenting with product diversification. They've been linking with each other to do benchmarking. The most progressive — among them Canada, the UK, Denmark, Sweden, France, Germany, the Netherlands, Australia, New Zealand — have launched diversified ventures and wholly-owned subsidiaries.

A few, like the Dutch, have complete commercial freedom through liberalization and privatization. The KPN acquisition of TNT is a formidable move on the competitive battlefield, and could not have been accomplished without the transformation which preceded. Germany may follow over the next few years, if it will divest shares. Others — Chile, Argentina, several Asian countries like Malaysia and Singapore — are well-positioned to absorb the lessons learned by the first group of progressives. But for all those countries there is, to date, a common postal environment: a basic universal postal service, parcels and letters distribution, and retail post offices. This won't last.

As events occur over the next few years, we anticipate divergence in the postal sector. In the near term, the fastest moving countries will be those like the Netherlands, Denmark, Sweden, New Zealand, Australia — who have already got a substantial degree of commercial freedom. They're relatively small. They're fast moving already. They've got good quality management. They're making money and can raise capital. And they've got visions about the future of the industry and their position within it. They'll be taking risks.

The United States and Canada may move more slowly than those countries. Despite their size and influence — unless given more commercial freedom — they may lose ground relative to the other players in the market. They will be focusing on building efficient pipelines to and from major trade areas to maximize the advantage of the North American customer base and market size.

Players also might emerge to open up niche positions in the marketplace on an international basis. We can't predict who they'll be, but we see the scope for international joint ventures broadening to open up specialist distribution products and services in the marketplace, both regionally and globally. That's the near term.

In the longer term, we'll see interesting developments through the World Bank postal reform program. This may well impact 30 to 35 countries — not an insignificant number who will be making radical changes in the way they run their postal operations and introducing new products. They'll do that through bringing in skills from foreign postal services or foreign private companies, and from receiving investments from those companies. Foreign postal services may invest in those countries, too, and consequently introduce further reforms back home as they learn how to profit in the global community. Of course, the increased competition from private companies in the developed world will stimulate further rapid changes within the foreign postal services.

Specifically, we could see significant positions being established in the global postal environment by both Germany and the UK, if they are divested (Germany is the more likely candidate, as we write). The pair's scale would make them formidable competitors or collaborators with smaller, fast moving players.

Volume should grow dramatically in emerging markets — China and India, in particular. Postal economic growth will also take place in the Asia Pacific region, paralleling the predicted economic growth, international trading patterns, and consumerism rising in that region.

With this change, niche players will appear over time and will specialize in different aspects of the postal marketplace: some focused on products, others on operations. The result will be greater competition, and a growing divergence between the sort of vibrant, successful smaller companies and the more lethargic, constrained larger national posts.

## The Big Questions

For the remainder of this chapter, we'll specifically address several of what we'll term the "big questions" — issues that will shape, both in the short and long terms, the directions in which the postal sector will move. For the short term, we are considering the next three years. For the long term, our perspective encompasses a decade.

## How Will the Balance Shift Between National and International Business?

Today, most posts' cash flows from their domestic letters businesses. But there are a number of postal services — especially those that have entered the remail market — which are making a large amount of their profit from international mail. Much of that mail is to and from a relatively small number of countries. As market liberalization takes hold, it first affects international transactions. With the accompanying changes in pricing arrangements for international mail, those profits may be lost.

If there's going to be a threat of lost profit from international transactions, posts will be inclined to collaborate with those representing their country's principal trading partners. However that collaboration may be complicated by terminal dues — the compensation that one post, say the U.S. Postal Service, will give to another, for example Deutsche Post, for the delivery of international mail sent from America. The U.S. Postal Service collects the cost of the letter's stamp, so it must provide the compensation.

In the past, terminal dues have been calculated on a basis that hasn't reflected true cost. Postal services have begun to introduce new arrangements which will more closely relate to cost. But this creates another problem. It removes the arbitrage opportunity that's been in the market, an opportunity that's become remail. Where a postal service has a high cost structure, the sending postal service now has a choice. It can either increase its tariff to the sending international mailers or it can try to find alternative delivery agents in the receiving countries and bypass the receiving postal system. It's easy to see some of this logic behind KPN's bid for TNT.

These developments are also driving concern about the reliability of international mail. And with good reason. Even in a country with quality domestic service, international mail transactions receive shorter shrift. As a result, there's action within many posts to try and improve the quality of that international mail system. Poor quality will mean they'll rapidly lose market share. Nevertheless, most posts will see continuing strong growth in the volume of international mail coupled with price reduction in the transactions over the next few years, because international trade is growing quickly.

In that near-term period, postal quality will improve dramatically on a number of the developed country routes, but competitors will also enter those markets. They'll aggressively target high-volume and high-density customers — those who are sending large volumes of transactions to small numbers of receivers. Even so, the domestic letter service will still provide dominant cash flows.

Ten years out, however, we could find that most business-to-business financial transactions and communications have converted into electronic form. There'll still be marketing mail activities, but most business invoicing transactions will have switched. Domestic and

still be marketing mail activities, but most business invoicing transactions will have switched. Domestic and international direct mail and catalogues will still be going strongly because the postal part of the advertising market will provide value. International home shopping and value-added package delivery services will be established and growing substantially, both for home and business deliveries. But there will be strong competition between the postal services, global courier companies and niche national distribution operators who seek to gain position in these new markets.

In conclusion, the segmentation of the postal business will have changed substantially by 2005. That's why postal services need to focus on utilization and implementation of technology for service improvement and value-added products and services.

### Where Will the Global Market Move?

Near-term growth will continue at historic rates, four to six percent by volume. Revenue growth — by contrast — will be dependent on tariff increases. Up to now, it's been  easy for postal services — either to finance inefficiencies or to support increased cash targets from their governments — to raise cash by raising the tariff.  As competition enters the sector and as the electronic alternative prices decline, that's an unsustainable position.

Long-term growth rates by volume will shrink, from four to six percent to less than two percent, as business transactions disappear. Absolute levels of revenue may decline. Volume growth will become dependent on direct mail and the resulting package delivery. This will lead to a major structural shift. Segmentation of business will occur: a decline in business-to-business mail, a decline in statements and invoices, a decline in per-

with substantial growth in business-to-consumer direct marketing in most countries.

In the United States that's already a well-established marketplace, but even that market could see growth as new flexible collection and delivery services are introduced. These link to electronic services and new software services, all positioned to take advantage of the vast delivery and retail networks.

Rates of growth will vary by region. North America will be slow because of the position already achieved in the United States and the difficulty for USPS to mobilize commercial development because of the opposition it suffers. In Europe, the European Community and the eventual deregulation of its postal markets will provide some significant growth of the market, but not in the short term. But the fastest growth will be in Asia Pacific where economies are booming.

## How Will the Competition React to the Sector's Transformation?

Competition will grow significantly, in the near term, slowly through the prospects of liberalization in Europe and further through de facto liberalization in other parts of the world. Substitute technology, particularly within financial services, will have impact. As market regulations open up, small companies will chip away legally at the edges of the postal services. They will be an irritant, tending to skim off attractive, profitable transactions. Within a city, for example, companies may begin to collect business mail from certain neighborhoods and provide a highly reliable same-day or next-day delivery service. Those companies may recruit the posts' best management talent, taking advantage of the fact that postal services typically cannot compete with private-sector top management compensation.

Competition from the couriers and the integrators, like Federal Express, will of course continue. And they'll combine fast and reliable services with new warehousing and distribution activities. New competition will emerge from specialist mail-order companies and direct marketers. They may choose to do some of the distribution themselves or join together and set up competing distribution companies.

Long-term, increasing crossborder activity from major customers will cause the postal services to compete more with each other. If a major customer is demanding a one-stop shop, then postal services will be selling this, offering delivery of items in other countries. They'll seek the best, most reliable deal — even if it means partnering with or acquiring private companies. In the most promising market segments, posts will create new companies operating domestically in foreign countries.

These efforts will lead to significant alliances between postal services and private sector organizations, especially in skill areas which posts need to acquire quickly. Partnerships with computing, software, systems, and high technology companies; with logistics businesses and couriers; and with customers will all address the need for more sophisticated skills.

The posts themselves will face off in high-density domestic traffic routes, on the most profitable international routes, and in attractive customer segments. In those countries where postal administrations have adopted commercial management practices and won commercial freedom, they will remain dominant.

## Will Transformation Bring New Players into the Postal Sector?

Courier companies will continue to enter parts of the postal market. Customer groups are already there: specialist mail-order companies are doing their own distribution. Publishers may enter, if they find it feasible to get magazines into subscribers' homes some other way, although a similar well-financed effort by the publishing industry in the United States did not significantly penetrate the market. Financial services companies may enter if they can provide lower-cost distribution electronically. Meanwhile, long-term, posts may enter foreign domestic markets. At the moment, foreign posts are operating in countries like the United States, to attract international traffic into their own network for delivery in other countries. When a postal service enters the domestic market in another country, that will be a moment of high drama. And it's coming.

## How Will Postal Customers — and Their Demands — Change?

Direct mail, particularly for financial services, publishing and mail-order companies, will grow short-term. Home shopping transactions will expand in response to new technology applications and changing consumer behavior. Where markets liberalize, telecommunications and perhaps broadcast television, mailing and billing activity to the home will also rise. That is, market liberalization and more widespread technology applications in the home lead to growth in overall communication, which leads to growth in direct mail advertising, which leads to growth in fulfillment mailing.

The posts' challenge will be to spot trends in emerging competition in markets and go for volume and value growth from those customer niches. The telecom market in Europe is liberalizing in 1998. In the United States it's also liberalizing. Those will be new mailing opportunities.

We're finding throughout the world a growth in the number of small businesses. Economic development is moving quickly and there's a lot of vibrancy within the medium scale marketplace. That will shift growth in mailing and parcels distribution.

In the longer term, we see sustained growth in transactions associated with the aging population: mailing home health care products, more home education as increased leisure time causes demand; more specialist financial services transactions. To capture those, postal services need to spot the trends and support the development of associated products.

Customer demands will change. Sending customers will want easier access, and billing to be user-friendly. They won't want complex transactions they don't understand. Sending customers will insist on ease of payment. They'll demand quality account management and customization of product packages. Sending customers will also require, as a pre-qualification, added value from high reliability, predictability, and speed offered in optional features. This combination of features will be the price of admission in the market, because the posts' competition will drive up quality and reliability, and drive down price over time.

Receiving customers will want fast receipt of ordered items within 24 hours. They'll want flexible delivery — possibly in the evenings or on weekends and holidays — and they will be willing to pay a premium for it. That will be a significant shift: historically, it has been the sending customer that pays for postal services, with the exception of mail order.

## How Will Posts' Relationships with Suppliers Be Affected?

In the next few years, posts' cost structures won't change much. Labor will be the greatest expense, followed by information systems, retail counters automation, materials handling mechanization, and automated equipment; land, buildings and their related costs; and vehicles. Ten years out, however, outsourcing or contracting out will be a key strategy that effects both overall costs, and relations with labor.

As networks grow more complicated, there will be new entrants — perhaps the big computer companies — to the automated sorting and equipment environments. Posts will be forming alliances with some suppliers.

Data network capacity will be purchased on a large scale. If posts are going to capture ubiquitous data and manage information concerning the transactions put through the physical network, they'll have to invest. This will introduce new skill needs and a new layer of complexity — one that's global, and not merely domestic, because customers will want to deal in a seamless way across the global environment.

## Which Substitute Technology Products Will Pose the Toughest Challenges?

Posts are already facing competition from the fax, e-mail, and electronic commerce transactions. But these communications are breeding more postal communications. For example, if a business advertises on television, the customer responses create new mailing lists, leading to secondary advertising. The new transactions are generating mail.

In the longer run, those technologies are going to survive and prosper. The Internet is going to have an increasing impact on postal services. It will substitute some transactions but also allow for growth in mailing and package delivery. We can't predict exactly what sorts of electronic products are going to be coming, but what we can be certain of is that business and commerce will grow and continue to create new opportunities for both posts (requiring physical delivery) and communications in general. There'll be lots of experimentation and the mass market will grow accustomed to using electronic transactions. However, the uncertainty that consumer electronic mail will be opened and acted upon, or even spotted by the targeted customer, in the Internet environment, will assure a viable channel for traditional mail. The key to the medium, be it electronic or physical, is the probability that the communication will be acted upon — one way or another — by the addressee.

### Will Letter Monopolies Remain Protected?

Yes, in the near term. In Europe, however, there's already a trend towards erosion of the end-to-end monopoly. We expect different segments of the marketplace that were formerly in the monopoly will be opened to competition. Parcels, for instance, have been liberalized in most countries for years now. Globally, the monopoly is typically defined by size, price, weight, content or a combination thereof. Whatever the definition, the level of protection is coming down.

With competition entering, postal services have to move quickly to be able to face up to this new and complex communications environment. The postal services can't rest on the fact that they've got a monopoly. They've got to start behaving competitively. As they do, posts will see it beneficial in the long run to have monopoly protection eased and perhaps even taken away in consideration for commercial freedom.

## Will Posts Continue to Operate Under a Universal Service Mandate (With or Without Monopoly Protection)?

Probably. Governments find the notion of the universal service obligation important and will use it as a quid pro quo for some monopoly protection. Where monopoly protection is taken away, postal services can usually negotiate some extra-commercial freedoms, but they will carry on with or without monopoly protection, we think, with an obligation to provide the universal service, as is the case in Sweden today.

The proportion of products going through the network that are not the universal minimum standard will grow over time. Discounting arrangements and higher-priced transactions are making the whole postal product mix much more complicated. The relevance of this universal service product will become less profound. The total amount of cost and revenues associated with it will be relatively small.

## Will the Tariff — or Stamp Price — Remain Uniform?

If it does, the services associated with it may not. The uniform tariff is inextricably linked to the universal service obligation. In the United States, for example, the basic cost of the first class stamp gets your letter anywhere you want it to go. That basic published tariff is likely to remain uniform and cheap; in fact, it could start to come down in real terms in some countries if regulators are insulated from countervailing demands from government treasuries for cash receipts driven by tariff increases. Governments in the past have wanted to make posts cash cows, essentially forms of indirect taxation.

Postal services, to survive, need to start reducing real tariffs as in New Zealand. Otherwise volumes are probably going to go down quickly. Higher volume customers will be receiving much better discounts in the long run. Regulators are going to be interested in postal services' pricing policies. Real prices may come down. That would still mean a uniform tariff but it might stay constant in absolute terms over years. Different product features will attract new pricing structures, and this — in the long run — will challenge the basis of the uniform tariff.

## Will Posts Continue to be Given Favorable Tax Treatment?

No, it's inevitable that posts will become treated just like any other company. It is in Australia. They are in Denmark and the UK. Postal services are exempt from the Value Added Tax in most of Europe, but that can't survive. The VAT exemption provides an unlevel playing field for competition. Different rules for the public provider and the private companies are unsustainable.

## Is There Labor Flexibility in Posts' Future?

There has to be. Postal working practices must become more flexible. If they don't and, in the worst case, a government carries on trying to increase tariffs, then the competitive viability of the services will be damaged. We're seeing difficulties in the UK in this area: tariffs are rising and labor relations hardening. It's happened before — in Canada, Australia, Denmark and elsewhere. The cost of labor, as a percentage of total costs, must decline through investments in technology, new workrule practices, cooperative approaches between labor and management, and team empowerment. All will result in improved productivity. Absent such changes, the posts cannot remain competitive.

## How Will Posts' Ownership Structure Change?

In the near term, strange as it may seem, the fastest changes will come in countries participating in the World Bank program, which will bring more private financing into the sector. Some of the big divestitures could happen in Germany, Italy, and possibly the UK. However, most of the postal administrations will remain in public ownership in the near term. But they will drive harder towards commercialization.

In the longer term, there may be a more radical shift in ownership driven by changes through mergers and acquisitions— with holding companies playing a role. There will be more joint ventures, government privatizations and cross shareholdings. There will be a slow but significant move towards privately-owned postal entities with outside shareholders.

## How Will Information Technology Develop?

Information technology currently exists as a second-class area in most postal services. That won't last. IT will rapidly assume a major importance in supporting operational networks, customer billing, marketing databases, and costing systems (to support pricing judgements and regulatory defenses). IT investment is required to address the need to add value, to overlay information management to the physical processing of mail and parcels, to interconnect with customers' IT environments, to manage marketing databases, and to have much better costing systems in order to understand how to price this new complicated product environment. Do postal services have the vision and skills to specify, buy and run this sort of environment? It's a big strategic issue for most.

Distribution's sorting and delivery will be increasingly integrated with the IT data network and customer systems. In the near term, the priority will be to improve the flexibility of sorting and help create competitive advantage through image capture.

Investment dollars are being directed to improving the flexibility of the whole sorting environment so as to reduce the cost of processing. In the longer run, we see this environment with much more mass data processing, image capture and links to other systems — geographic information, customer billing — so, in interpreting the data, choices can be made on which kinds of product features to offer to the customers. It is conceivable that in the process of high-speed image capture, linked to communications systems, posts will know the precise location of every mail piece every minute, every day. That would completely change the nature of the competitive environment. Why would any customer pay ten, 20 or 30 times the cost of regular first-class mail for courier service, if a post could track every piece and offer highly predictable service?

## Will the Postal Sector Be Besieged by Mergers and Acquisitions?

Not by many full mergers, but more likely by cross-border, multi-party ventures. In the short term, there will be both operational technology and customer joint ventures and alliances, domestically and internationally. And they will have several purposes: to protect certain types of business, to acquire needed skill sets, to incorporate new senior management, to reduce cost and to enter new markets.

Longer term, some postal services will be active in buying and/or operating other country's postal services as they go through privatization. They'll take up management contracts. They'll acquire electronics, software, home shopping, courier and niche telecom companies.

## Who Will Be the Big Winners in Market Share and Profitability?

That's the biggest of the big questions. Near term, it will be the posts who already have commercial freedom. The Netherlands, Denmark, Sweden, New Zealand and Australia are all potential winners because they're small enough to operate nimbly and profitably with a visionary perspective. If they get commercial freedom, Canada and the United States will become big winners in the future too. In the United States, even a small, compounded annual growth creates new business that represents more volume and revenue than the totals in many developed countries.

Longer term, the big winners will include the beneficiaries of the World Bank investment program, Germany and the United Kingdom (if they're divested), and China and India, because of their high-volume potential.

## Back to the Future

In the Swiss auditorium last April, before the world's postal administrators, the World Bank's Kumar Ranganathan also remained cautiously optimistic. In many countries, he noted, "the postal sector is at a critical juncture."

"If nothing is done," warned Ranganathan, as we first noted in Chapter Two, "and the status quo is maintained, then it is likely that the sector will continue to erode as competitors and other communications media take over the market. Under such a situation, it may not be possible to provide a postal service at a reasonable cost or to ensure universal service. Given the importance of this sector, particularly in developing countries, such a situation would lead to adversity in the net welfare.

"However," he added, "countries that commit themselves to postal reform could turn their postal service around so that it becomes an important player in the communications market. The benefits of a carefully planned and well-executed reform program can be significant."

The gauntlet had been thrown. Let the transformation spread.

# Afterword

## Looking to the Future

_____

BY THOMAS E. LEAVEY,
DIRECTOR GENERAL OF THE
INTERNATIONAL BUREAU OF THE
UNIVERSAL POSTAL UNION

Postal services do not operate in a vacuum. They are services which influence — and are in return influenced by — a series of social and economic factors. In the same way postal activities affect the economy, the economy has an impact on the level of postal activity in a given country. One elementary indicator of this phenomenon is the postal consumption count, the number of postal articles posted per capita per annum. This figure varies from under five in some developing regions to over 700 in some developed countries. Other important indicators are literacy rates, and geographic and demographic figures.

The level of demand, and the degree of sophistication with which this demand is satisfied, tend to divide the postal world into different categories, much like football teams in different leagues. Yet, unlike football teams, the postal services of the world must play together. Greater harmonization, more uniformity and better use of our extensive postal network are goals toward which all of us should strive. But we have also seen that these goals are difficult to achieve.

In spite of the rather wide diversity among postal services, there are some trends which seem to stand out, and which promise to have global implications for postal services in the long run. Much of what is happening on the postal scene is the product of the rapid disappearance of the status quo to which postal services were accustomed over a long period of time. There is no going back from this position; we can only go forward.

What are these trends? Globalization, a diminishing monopoly, changing national economies, a "buyer's market", and the development of new technologies.

## Globalization

The landscape of global business has changed. Globalization, although it is still something of a catchword today, will progressively become a central feature of all businesses, including postal services. With falling trade barriers, the expanding liberalization of markets, and dramatic improvements in communication infrastructure, businesses will not only face greater competition within their national borders, but will also seek new opportunities in international markets. Postal administrations will no longer be able to hide behind closed domestic markets protected by the postal monopoly.

## Diminishing Monopoly

The trend toward diminishing monopolies in the postal market will continue, driven by multiple factors exerting strong influence on policy-makers. Among these factors are the emergence of the private sector as a dominant force in the transportation and communications sector; lobbying groups established by the private couriers which, through claims that a level playing field is needed, are actively pushing to reduce the postal monopoly to a bare minimum; the more recent orientation of financial and development agencies like the World Bank and the International Monetary Fund as advocates of less government control and more private initiative; and — in Europe especially, through the regulatory influence exercised by the European Union — the liberalization of telecommunications and postal markets. In its proposed directives on liberalization of the postal market, the EU wants to set limits on the postal monopoly and to harmonize the common universal service obligations of its members. The issues raised, although particular to the member countries of the EU, will certainly have an influence far beyond the European sphere.

## National Economies

Postal business is closely linked to the health of national economies. Successful postal reform movements, therefore, will be linked to reform movements in other sectors of national economies which attract new business. If the national economy is strong, more postal traffic will be generated. But it is also true that if economies have high labor costs, high taxes or high postage rates, postal traffic will tend to migrate toward economies that can offer a better quality/cost ratio. With globalization and the liberalization of markets, the international postal business will inevitably become more mobile.

## Buyer's Market

The postal industry has entered into a "buyer's market" phase. Customers have become very demanding and are no longer satisfied with existing standards of reliability, economy and service. They want faster, more reliable postal service. They want customized products that suit their needs. The list of customer needs and expectations is long: more and better information concerning foreign mailing lists and postal codes, time-certain delivery, delivery confirmation, EDI interfaces for payment, and track and trace facilities for items and for entire shipments. What will happen if the industry can't fill those needs? Postal customers will simply look elsewhere.

In a buyer's market, competitors become options. Postal services will need to find new ways of positioning themselves as an attractive option for tomorrow's demanding customers. What will the options be for buyers over the next few years? Express carriers, mail consolidators, remailers, even other international postal services will compete with the national postal service provider for larger parts of their core business, physical mail. And electronic communication providers are reaching today well beyond their national borders to form partnerships on a truly global scale. If they are not already there, they will soon be poised to take an even larger share of the market that was once reserved for the mails.

## Technological Development

The fast pace of technological development is another trend that must be addressed. Technology certainly will continue to be used by postal services as a generator of growth for physical mail. Many postal services have proven that they can use technology to create new postal products and to improve their infrastructure, distribution network, and the information they provide customers about their mail shipments. With technology, they have been able to hold down operating costs and improve their quality of service. Of course, this means greater customer satisfaction and more mail. In the coming years, we can expect to see these technological improvements spreading to more of the developing countries.

But increasingly, technology will also be used as a substitute for physical mail. The communications market as a whole is experiencing explosive growth. Physical mail will hold just one small share of that expanding market. The impact of the use of fax and electronic mail is already evident. The presence of other forms of electronic communication such as interactive cable TV and the Internet will also increase. One outcome is abundantly clear: the postal industry is beginning to move out of the letter business and into the message business. Some postal services will see this as an opportunity to diversify into new business markets. Others, I am afraid, will miss out on the opportunity.

The explosive growth of the communications market will also force more postal services to move beyond their core, the physical mail business. They will have to begin to diversify in order to broaden the range of choices they offer their customers. Some of these new hybrid postal products, which combine electronics with hardcopy delivery, are already being used successfully today by the more innovative postal services.

In the end, change and reform will be the crucial elements for ensuring postal growth. A growing number of postal services have shown that reform works. The Universal Postal Union will have to concentrate its efforts on convincing all postal services that their future depends on their willingness to begin the postal reform process. Taking a proactive approach gives postal services the means to anticipate future changes as they embark on, or continue, their transformation.

*Thomas E Leavey is the Director-General of the International Bureau of the Universal Postal Union, a post he was elected to in 1994 at the 21st Universal Postal Congress in Seoul, Republic of Korea.*

*Director-General Leavey is responsible for providing leadership in responding to the significant challenges the UPU faces as it approaches the next century. These include the increasing liberalization of postal services, the need to adopt more customer-oriented commercial integration of developing countries into the universal postal network.*

*Director-General Leavey is the former Assistant Postmaster General, responsible for International Postal Affairs, of the United States Postal Service. He held that post from 1987 until his election, and supervised the development, execution and management of all the elements of the USPS's international mail business, including sales and promotion, service pricing and negotiations, and geographic and targeted marketing activities.*

*As head of the United States delegation to various UPU and other international meetings on postal matters, Director-General Leavey made valuable contributions to global cooperation among postal administrations. He was also selected by his peers in the USPS and UPU to serve on many important working parties and committees. In recognition of his outstanding achievement in ensuring the successful hosting of the 1989 UPU Congress in Washington, D.C., Director-General Leavey received the John Wanamaker Award, the highest distinction given to an officer of the USPS.*

*A 1968 graduate of Princeton University, Director-General Leavey joined the United States Postal Service in 1970.*

# INDEX